SSR Paper 20

The Nexus Between Security Sector Governance/Reform and Sustainable Development Goal-16: An Examination of Conceptual Linkages and Policy Recommendations

DCAF-Commissioned SSR Policy Paper
Oya Dursun-Özkanca

]u[
ubiquity press
London

DCAF
Geneva Centre
for Security Sector
Governance
DCAF
Geneva

Published by
Ubiquity Press Ltd.
Unit 322–323
Whitechapel Technology Centre
75 Whitechapel Road
London E1 1DU
www.ubiquitypress.com

First published 2021

Cover photograph: Aubrey Wade, Panos Pictures
Cover photograph description: Winnefred, a Liberian National Police (LNP) officer, tells Itee, a female peacekeeping soldier belonging to the all-female unit of Indian UN peacekeepers in Monrovia, about the ingredients used in local dishes while out on a Joint Task Force (JTF) patrol in the Duport Road area.

Print and digital versions typeset by Siliconchips Services Ltd.

ISBN (Paperback): 978-1-911529-96-5
ISBN (PDF): 978-1-911529-97-2
ISBN (EPUB): 978-1-911529-98-9
ISBN (Mobi): 978-1-911529-99-6

Series: SSR Papers
ISSN (Print): 2571-9289
ISSN (Online): 2571-9297

DOI: https://doi.org/10.5334/bcm

The full text of this book has been peer-reviewed to ensure high academic standards. For full review policies, see https://www.ubiquitypress.com/

Suggested citation:
Dursun-Özkanca, O. 2021. *The Nexus Between Security Sector Governance/Reform and Sustainable Development Goal-16: An Examination of Conceptual Linkages and Policy Recommendations*. London: Ubiquity Press. DOI: https://doi.org/10.5334/bcm. License: CC-BY-NC

Correction (23 June 2021):
Page 59, paragraph 2 of the originally published manuscript has been updated. The concept of "trilemma" was incorrectly attributed to Gill (2020). In the updated version of the manuscript, the concept of "trilemma" was correctly attributed to Cayford, Pieters & Hijzen (2018). A missing reference to Gill (2020) was also added to the References list.

To read the free, open access version of this book online, visit https://doi.org/10.5334/bcm or scan this QR code with your mobile device:

Table of Contents

List of Tables

Dedication

To my parents, Dr. Gönül Oya Dursun (1944–2017) and Dr. Yunus Dursun, for serving as great role models and believing in me.

SSR Papers

The DCAF SSR Papers provide original, innovative and provocative analysis on the challenges of security sector governance and reform. Combining theoretical insight with detailed empirically-driven explorations of state-of-the-art themes, SSR Papers bridge conceptual and pragmatic concerns. Authored, edited and peer reviewed by SSR experts, the series provides a unique platform for in-depth discussion of a governance-driven reform agenda, addressing the overlapping interests of researchers, policy-makers and practitioners in the fields of development, peace and security.

DCAF, the Geneva Centre for Security Sector Governance, is dedicated to making states and people safer. Good security sector governance, based on the rule of law and respect for human rights, is the very basis of development and security. DCAF assists partner states in developing laws, institutions, policies and practices to improve the governance of their security sector through inclusive and participatory reforms based on international norms and good practices.

About the Author

Dr. Oya Dursun-Özkanca (University of Texas at Austin, Ph.D.) is Endowed Chair of International Studies and Professor of Political Science at Elizabethtown College. Her research interests include transatlantic security, European Union, South East Europe, Eastern Mediterranean, and peace operations. She is the author of *Turkey–West Relations: The Politics of Intra-alliance Opposition* (Cambridge University Press, 2019). She is also the editor of *The European Union as an Actor in Security Sector Reform* (Routledge, 2014) and *External Interventions in Civil Wars* (co-edited with Stefan Wolff, Routledge, 2014). Her articles appeared in *Foreign Policy Analysis*, *Civil Wars*, *European Security*, and *Ethnopolitics*, among others.

Declaration

The views expressed in this publication do not in any way reflect the opinion or views of DCAF, the Geneva Centre for Security Sector Governance.

This book has been peer reviewed by multiple experts within the subject area. One of these peer reviewers is employed by DCAF but was not part of the editorial processes.

Acknowledgements

I am thankful for the love and support of my husband Kemal and my sons Bora and Tolan, which kept me strong and centered during the writing process of this manuscript throughout the COVID-19 lockdown. I would like to thank William McDermott, Alexandra Preperier, Merle Jasper, and the two anonymous peer reviewers for giving me such constructive and helpful feedback on my manuscript. I also would like to express my deepest gratitude to Dr. Wayne Selcher for reading this manuscript in its entirety and helping me edit it. Parts of the penultimate chapter were published in Dursun-Özkanca, O 2018 The European Union rule of law mission in Kosovo: An analysis from the local perspective. *Ethnopolitics*, 17(1): 71–94.

Executive Summary

This Security Sector Reform (SSR) Paper offers a universal and analytical perspective on the linkages between Security Sector Governance (SSG)/SSR (SSG/R) and Sustainable Development Goal-16 (SDG-16), focusing on conflict and post-conflict settings as well as transitional and consolidated democracies. Against the background of development and security literatures traditionally maintaining separate and compartmentalized presence in both academic and policymaking circles, it maintains that the contemporary security- and development-related challenges are inextricably linked, requiring effective measures with an accurate understanding of the nature of these challenges. In that sense, SDG-16 is surely a good step in the right direction. This manuscript attempts to bridge the gap between the development and security literatures by offering a conceptual framework for the interlinkages between SSG/R with SDG-16, tying the two together more closely using human security as a linkage. After comparing and contrasting SSG/R and SDG-16, this manuscript argues that human security lies at the heart of the nexus between the *2030 Agenda* of the United Nations (UN) and SSG/R. It highlights the importance of the principles of democratic oversight and accountability as well as a participative approach and local ownership in making sure that SSR effectively contributes to the accomplishment of SDG-16 targets.

Oya Dursun-Özkanca
College Professor of International Studies,
Endowed Chair
Professor of Political Science
Elizabethtown College
Elizabethtown, PA, USA

CHAPTER 1

Introduction

Development and security literatures have traditionally maintained a separate and compartmentalized presence in both academic and policymaking circles. Nevertheless, contemporary security- and development-related challenges rarely occur in isolation and they are inextricably linked. Failed and failing states, ethno-nationalist and religious extremist ideologies, extreme poverty, corruption, organized crime, displacement, refugees, and environmental issues pose complex challenges to individuals, societies, as well as the international community – that is, international and regional organizations as well as their member states, requiring effective measures and an accurate understanding of the nature of these challenges.

To illustrate, at the end of 2019, about 736 million people (10% of the world's population) lived in extreme poverty, about 821 million were malnourished, and about 30% of young women and 13% of young men were not enrolled in education (United Nations General Assembly [UNGA] 2019: 25). According to the UN High Commissioner on Refugees (UNHCR), 79.5 million people were forced to flee their homes due to 'persecution, conflict, violence, human rights violations or events seriously disturbing public order' (2020: 2). The aggregate forcible displacement figure in the last 10 years is over 100 million people (UNHCR 2020). Climate change and food insecurity are expected to become major drivers of conflicts and displacement, as about 350 million people are affected by climate change-related disasters, 'reversing hard-won development gains and exacerbating poverty' (UN Secretary-General [UNSG] 2019: 7; UNHCR 2020). 'As these and other problems persist and proliferate, we see growing fear, uncertainty and frustration undermining public trust in institutions and political establishments,' creating a 'breeding ground for hate speech, xenophobia and other divisive and dangerous narratives' (UNGA 2019: 7).

Moreover, many countries around the world were already struggling to meet the Sustainable Development Goals (SDGs), particularly SDG-16, before COVID-19 (Sachs et al. 2019). Responses to COVID-19 have further illustrated the existing patterns of systemic social and economic inequalities, disparities in access to resources, discrimination, and intolerance, and demonstrated how interconnected the environment, economy, employment, and health

How to cite this book chapter:
Dursun-Özkanca, O. 2021. *The Nexus Between Security Sector Governance/Reform and Sustainable Development Goal-16: An Examination of Conceptual Linkages and Policy Recommendations.* Pp. 1–9. London: Ubiquity Press. DOI: https://doi.org/10.5334/bcm.a. License: CC-BY-NC

and well-being are. As noted in the UN's *Shared Responsibility, Global Solidarity* report published in response to the COVID-19 pandemic (UN 2020c: 8), the developing world will particularly experience additional setbacks, as the pandemic 'will further weaken an already fragile macroeconomic picture, where debt accumulation has outpaced the growth of income even before the crisis.' The same report warns that 'conflicts prevent effective measures for fighting COVID-19,' and 'those in conflict areas are most at risk of suffering devastating loss from COVID-19' (UN 2020c: 12). For instance, the pandemic has augmented the power of criminal networks in Brazil (Berg & Varsori 2020) and increased democratic backsliding and draconian measures in the Western Balkans (Wunsch 2020). It created a 'shadow pandemic,' by causing increased violence against women and girls (Azcona et al. 2020: 21). The pandemic is also expected to reverse 'decades of progress in the fight against poverty,' and exacerbate 'already high levels of inequality within and between states' (UN 2020c: 8).

Due to the interconnected nature of security and development, such complex challenges require a multifaceted yet coordinated response from all stakeholders at the international, national, and local levels. Just like it is not possible to have peace and security without sustainable economic development, it is not feasible to have sustainable economic development without peace and security. By including Goal 16, Peace, Justice and Strong Institutions among its SDGs as part of its *Agenda 2030*, the UN signaled that there is more to be done to link security and development around the world (UNGA 2015). The full title of SDG-16 – 'Promote peaceful and inclusive societies for sustainable development, provide access to justice for all and build effective, accountable and inclusive institutions at all levels' (UNGA 2015: 14) – aptly signifies the importance of the linkages among peace, security, justice, accountability, inclusivity, and sustainable development. As noted in *Agenda 2030*, 'the interlinkages and integrated nature of the Sustainable Development Goals are of crucial importance in ensuring that the purpose of the new Agenda is realized' (UNGA 2015: 2).

There are significant links between SSG/R and SDG-16. While SDG-16 contains numerous targets related to SSG/R, its targets are not solely about the security sector and includes significant references to sustainable development. SSR is increasingly employed as an approach to postconflict reconstruction and democratic transitions. While the SSR literature mainly focuses on post-conflict contexts (Dursun-Özkanca 2017), SSG has a broader application around the world and is pertinent to all countries. As the developments in the United States (US) following the murders of Breonna Taylor, George Floyd, Rayshard Brooks, and Daniel Prude under police custody revealed, not even the most advanced democracies in the world are exempt from structural deficiencies and systemic racism in the security sector. The rapid spread of international protests especially in response to the Floyd murder has underlined the urgent need for universally addressing institutionalized manifestations of racism and discrimination. Furthermore, the overwhelmingly disproportionate use of force against peaceful protestors revealed that even the most advanced democracies around the world would benefit from SSR and respecting good governance principles, such as accountability, which are advocated by SSG. To illustrate, in July and August 2020, the Trump Administration deployed US federal forces without name tags, even initially without identifying insignia, to a number of cities, such as Chicago, Portland, and Albuquerque in response to the peaceful protests. This raised significant concerns about transparency and accountability (*Connecticut Law Tribune*, 6 August 2020), as well as the application of 'human rights principles of necessity, proportionality, legality, and accountability for the use of crowd-control weapons' (Heisler, Mishori & Haar 2020). Furthermore, the US Government Accountability Office recently agreed to review matters related to the US federal government's use of 'less-lethal weapons and tactics,' such as the consideration of the use of a heat ray on peaceful protesters (Temple-Raston 2020). This renewed the public debate on the disproportionate of the use of force by the police.

Therefore, a universal and comprehensive analysis of the linkages between SSG/R and Sustainable Development Goal-16 (SDG-16) is called for. For this purpose, the current manuscript expands the focus on the study of the SSG/R-SDG-16 nexus to include a variety of contexts – conflict and post-conflict settings as well as transitional and consolidated democracies. This manuscript attempts to bridge the gap between the development and security literatures by exploring the conceptual and analytical linkages between SSG/R and SDG-16 to determine how SSG/R and SDG-16 are interlinked.

a. A roadmap

This manuscript offers a conceptual framework for the linkages between SSG/R and SDG-16, proposes new ways of looking at this relationship, and seeks to tie the two more closely by using human security as a bond. To do so, it first provides a brief overview of the scholarly and policymaking literature on the development-security nexus to set the background for the adoption of *The Agenda 2030*. Next, it reviews the literature on SSG/R and SDGs, and how each concept evolved over time. It then identifies the puzzle this study seeks to address by comparing and contrasting SSG/R with SDG-16. After making a case that human security lies at the heart of the nexus between the UN's *2030 Agenda* and SSG/R, this manuscript then analyses the strengths and weaknesses of human security as a bridge between SSG/R and SDG-16 and makes policy recommendations on how SSG/R, bolstered by human security, may help achieve better results on the SDG-16 targets. It specifically emphasizes the importance of transparency, oversight, and accountability on the one hand, and participative approach and local ownership on the other. It concludes by arguing that a simultaneous emphasis on security and development is sorely needed for addressing the issues under the purview of SDG-16.

b. The security-development nexus

The security-development nexus is not necessarily something new. The founders of the Bretton Woods system recognized it back in the 1940s (Zoellick 2008). In fact, in founding the International Bank for Reconstruction and Development (IBRD), which later has become the World Bank (WB) Group, they noted, 'Programs of reconstruction and development will speed economic progress everywhere, will aid political stability and foster peace' (The US Department of State Bulletin 1944: 114). Drawing on the same recognition, Rostow (1971) proposed a universalist model that perceives all nations rationally pursuing the goals of industrialization and material security, thereby lessening the causes of social conflict and promoting political stability. Rostow's 'optimistic philosophy is captured in US President John F. Kennedy's motto "a rising tide lifts all boats," which saw economic strategies overcoming racial and social inequalities domestically and development inequalities internationally' (Pupavac 2010: 696). Nevertheless, it is important to note that Rostow's theory has been criticized for its Westernized and neo-colonialist features (Jacobs 2015).

Development and security are essential for economic, social, and political stability. There is an important relationship between poverty, corruption, mismanagement of resources, and justice (UK Department for International Development [UK DFID] 2009). Having a well-functioning rule of law is necessary for sustaining peace and security. There are 'negative consequences of insecurity on poverty reduction efforts' (Bergenas & Mahoney 2016). Therefore, solely devoting attention to national economic development without security concerns might exacerbate insecurities that are already existent (Boyce 2002; Maresko 2004; Uvin 1998). While insecurity destroys the economic and political structure of a country, it also damages the access to justice.

The difference between negative and positive peace emerges as important to address at this conjuncture. In one of the earliest studies on the security-development nexus, Galtung (1964) defines negative peace as 'the absence of violence, absence of war,' and positive peace as 'the integration of human society.' The latter proves to serve as an important connection between the development and security spheres, as it contains 'the attitudes, institutions and structures that create and sustain peaceful societies' (Institute for Economics & Peace [IEP] 2020: 54). There are eight pillars of positive peace: 'well-functioning government, sound business environment, accepting the rights of others, good relations with neighbors, free flow of information, high levels of human capital, low levels of corruption, and equitable distribution of resources,' which make the connection between development and security clear (IEP 2020: 55).

Since the 1990s, there has been an increasing number of scholars and international organizations that recognize the interconnectedness among development and peace and security. Many scholars argued that the provision of security is a precondition for development and well-being (Krause & Jütersonke 2005; Schwarz 2005). Nevertheless, in the last decade or so, the international community has gradually started to view security and development as mutually reinforcing areas and acknowledged the need to achieve development and security concurrently, rather than addressing one as a precondition for addressing the other. A quick overview of the major policy papers and reports adopted by the leading international organizations over time effectively illustrates this observation. International organizations, such as the United Nations (UN), the WB, the Organisation for Economic Co-operation and Development (OECD), and the European Union (EU), all published key documents that led the way for the international community to acknowledge the interconnected nature of security/peace and development.

c. United Nations' approach to the security-development nexus

In 1992, in his *An Agenda for Peace* report, then UN Secretary-General (UNSG) Boutros-Ghali (UNSG 1992) encouraged the international security architectures to respond to the challenges of post-conflict reconstruction in the aftermath of the Cold War. This generated the multidimensional or integrated peacebuilding missions, such as the ones in Bosnia and Herzegovina, Kosovo, Haiti, Afghanistan, Liberia, Democratic Republic of Congo, Central African Republic, Timor-Leste, and Sierra Leone. The multidimensional or integrated peacebuilding missions are complex missions that aim at restoring the political, economic, and social infrastructures in post-conflict societies to establish governance and the rule of law, as well as social justice and economic development (Benner & Rotmann 2008; Dursun-Özkanca 2016). For example, a number of EU missions, such as the ones in Bosnia and Herzegovina, Macedonia, and Georgia, are aimed at SSR (especially capacity-building in relation to police forces and border guards) and others, such as the ones in Kosovo and Georgia, aim at the development of the rule of law. The UN mission to East Timor was perhaps the most 'ambitious' of these complex operations 'as it aimed at building a new state, enabling East Timor's transition from a territory occupied by Indonesia to a full-fledged member of the international community of sovereign states' (Caplan 2005; Wolff & Dursun-Özkanca 2012: 302).

Agenda for Peace contextualized the changing international environment in the immediate aftermath of the Cold War and acknowledged that the 'sources of conflict and war are pervasive and deep' and that they require the international community's 'utmost effort to enhance respect for human rights and fundamental freedoms, [and] to promote sustainable economic and social development for wider prosperity' (UNSG 1992: Paragraph 5). Referring to the 'complex' concept of international security and underlining the nexus between security and development, Boutros-Ghali noted, 'Poverty, disease, famine, oppression and despair … are both sources and consequences of conflict that require the ceaseless attention and the highest priority in the efforts of the United Nations' (UNSG 1992: Paragraph 13).

Additionally, *An Agenda for Development* (UNSG 1994) in 1994 and *the Brahimi Report* in 2000 represent some of the earlier attempts on the part of the UN to encourage a better alignment of the UN's security and development responsibilities for enhancing its performance in peace-making, peacekeeping, and post-conflict reconstruction (Tschirgi 2005). In *Agenda for Development*, Boutros-Ghali referred to development as 'a fundamental human right' and underlined that 'development is the most secure basis for peace' (UNSG 1994: Paragraph 3) but also went on to declare development to be 'in crisis' (UNSG 1994: Paragraph 5). He referred to 'peace as the foundation' of development, noting that 'Development cannot proceed easily in societies where military concerns are at or near the centre of life' (UNSG 1994: Paragraph 17). He maintained that in the absence of peace, countries may 'devote a higher percentage of their budget to the military than to development needs in health, education and housing' as 'preparation for war absorbs inordinate resources and impedes the development of social institutions' (UNSG 1994: Paragraph 17).

In 2005, *In Larger Freedom: Towards Development, Security and Human Rights for All*, then UN Secretary-General Kofi Annan underlined the importance of the connections between development, security, and human rights by referring to the concept of 'a larger freedom,' noting that it 'encapsulates the idea that development, security and human rights go hand in hand' (UNSG 2005: 5). In the same report, Annan (UNSG 2005: 5–6) continued to argue:

> Accordingly, we will not enjoy development without security, we will not enjoy security without development, and we will not enjoy either without respect for human rights. Unless all these causes are advanced, none will succeed. In this new millennium, the work of the United Nations must move our world closer to the day when all people have the freedom to choose the kind of lives they would like to live, the access to the resources that would make those choices meaningful and the security to ensure that they can be enjoyed in peace.

Annan added, 'Extreme poverty has many causes, ranging from adverse geography through poor or corrupt governance (including neglect of marginalized communities) to the ravages of conflict and its aftermath' (UNSG: 12). Referring to the concept of 'poverty traps,' Annan argued that many of the world's poorest countries are left 'languishing in a vicious circle of destitution,' and 'these countries cannot afford the basic investments needed to move onto a new path of prosperity unless they receive sustained, targeted external support' (UNSG 2005: 12).

Finally, as the mandate of the Millennium Development Goals (MDGs) was set to expire in 2015, the UN adopted *The 2030 Agenda for Sustainable Development*, which contains 17 SDGs (UNGA 2015). *Agenda 2030* is 'the result of over two years of intensive public consultation and engagement with civil society and other stakeholders around the world, which paid particular attention to the voices of the poorest and most vulnerable' (UNGA 2015: 3). Through *Agenda 2030*, between 2015 and 2030, the UN resolves to:

> end poverty and hunger everywhere; to combat inequalities within and among countries; to build peaceful, just and inclusive societies; to protect human rights and promote gender equality and the empowerment of women and girls; and to ensure the lasting protection of the planet and its natural resources … [and] to create conditions for sustainable, inclusive and sustained economic growth, shared prosperity and decent work for all, taking into account different levels of national development and capacities (UNGA 2015: 3).

Agenda 2030 aims to address factors that lead to violence, insecurity, injustice, inequality, corruption, poor governance, and illicit financial and arms flows (UNGA 2015). SDG-16 emerges as particularly key to this agenda. Very much like *In Larger Freedom*, *Agenda 2030* notes, 'Sustainable development cannot be realized without peace and security; and peace and security will be at risk without sustainable development' (UNGA 2015: 9). Through SDG-16, it acknowledges the importance of building 'peaceful, just, and inclusive societies that provide equal access to justice and that are based on respect for human rights (including the right to development), on effective rule of law and good governance at all levels and on transparent, effective and accountable institutions' (UNGA 2015: 9). Inclusivity is key, especially of women and youth. *Agenda 2030* notes, 'We must redouble our efforts to resolve or prevent conflict and to support post-conflict countries, including through ensuring that women have a role in peacebuilding and state-building' (UNGA 2015: 9).

d. Other international organizations' approaches to the security-development nexus

Besides the UN, the OECD has been a leading international actor on the security-development nexus, as it highlights the relationship between SSR and sustainable development. The SSR concept itself has been regularly promoted by its Development Assistance Committee (OECD-DAC), which has 30 member states that work on development cooperation, performance monitoring, and assessment (OECD 2020a). Indicative of the importance attributed to the security-development nexus, OECD-DAC's work on SSR, accountability, and democratic governance, poverty reduction, and effective donor policies has been influential in determining the accepted standards of behavior in the fields of peace/security and development. OECD-DAC has promoted SSR, leading to SSR's legitimization as a 'development activity' (Baldassini et al. 2018: 43). For the 2018–2022 period, for instance, OECD-DAC announced its goal as the promotion of 'development co-operation and other relevant policies' in service of the implementation of the *2030 Agenda*, through 'sustained, inclusive and sustainable economic growth, poverty eradication, [and] improvement of living standards in developing countries' (OECD 2020a).

The WB similarly emphasizes the linkages between security and development. To illustrate, in the aftermath of the Arab Spring, it issued its World Development Report (WB 2011), focusing on the nexus between conflict, security, and development. In its 2017 World Development Report, it emphasized the impact of good governance on reducing violence through 'effective deterrence, equitable distribution of resources, and legitimate dispute resolution' (Bisca 2018). More recently, the WB engaged in a greater synergy with the UN. The two organizations published the *Securing Development* report in 2017 and the *Pathways for Peace* document in 2018 (UN-WB 2018). The *Securing Development* report called for financial transparency and oversight on expenses over security and justice institutions and proposed expenditure analysis in SSR missions (Harborne et al. 2017).

In *Pathways for Peace*, the UN and WB (2018) argue that the prevention of conflict contributes to development progress. Subsequently, they recommend increased collaboration between the security and development circles and advocate that development actors should 'provide more support to national and regional prevention agendas through targeted, flexible, and sustained engagement,' and that 'Prevention agendas, in turn, should be integrated into development policies and efforts, because prevention is cost-effective, saves lives, and safeguards development gains' (UN and WB 2018: xviii). The *Pathways for Peace* further endorses investing in 'inclusive and sustainable development,' and argues, 'addressing inequalities and exclusion, making institutions more inclusive, and ensuring that development strategies are risk-informed are central to preventing the fraying of the social fabric that could erupt into crisis' (UN and WB 2018: xviii). Accordingly, there is now a formal partnership between the WB Group and the UN, titled The World Bank Group-UN Partnership Framework for Crisis-Affected Situations, which focuses on over 40 countries facing fragility, conflict, and violence (Bousquet 2019).

The EU has been another leading international actor when it comes to the security-development nexus. As it emerges as a leading actor in SSR (Sedra 2006a; Dursun-Özkanca 2012; 2014), it highlights the importance of a 'holistic' rather than a 'piece-by-piece approach adopted by other actors, such as NATO and its predominant focus on defence reform' (Dursun-Özkanca & Vandemoortele 2012: 145). In 2000, the EU outlined a number of priority areas of civilian action with an emphasis on SSR. These priority areas included police reform, the rule of law, strengthening of civilian administrations, and civil protection (Dursun-Özkanca & Vandemoortele 2012). In 2003, *the European Security Strategy* explicitly referred to SSR as a priority for the EU and also noted, 'Security is the first condition for development. Diplomatic efforts, development, trade and environmental policies, should follow the same agenda' (The Council of the EU 2003: 13). In 2005, the EU adopted the EU Concept for ESDP Support to Security Sector Reform, identifying the main guidelines for EU's engagement in SSR (CEU 2005). In 2016, the *European Union Global Strategy* document made references to SSR and the need to 'deliver security within the rule of law' (European External Action Service [EEAS] 2016: 26). In its 2019 update on its Global Strategy implementation, the EU referred to its involvement in the Tunisian and the Iraqi SSR processes (EEAS 2019). The EU holds that the security-development nexus is central for the success of reconstruction efforts. The EU's Africa Peace Facility, a major financial instrument to support cooperation with Africa on matters related to peace and security, is a good illustration of how the EU links development and security with an emphasis on peace, safety, security, political stability, effective governance, and sustainable and inclusive growth (European Commission 2019).

e. The security-development nexus debate in academia and policymaking

As is the case with the key documents adopted by international organizations on the security-development nexus, many scholars acknowledge that development and security reinforce each other and that they 'need to go hand in hand' (Duffield 2001; Zoellick 2008: 5). Just recently, in December 2020, the UN Security Council (UNSC) adopted Resolution 2553, 'stressing that reforming the security sector in post-conflict environments is critical to the consolidation of peace and stability, promoting poverty reduction, rule of law and good governance, extending legitimate State authority, and preventing countries from relapsing into conflict,' and that 'a professional, effective, and accountable security sector and accessible and impartial law-enforcement and justice sectors are equally necessary to laying the foundations for peace and sustainable development' (UNSC 2020b). The logic is that development enhances security as a result of peace dividends and that security makes longer-term development possible. The argument here is that violence is linked to 'poverty, inequality, and absence of opportunities' (Collinson et al. 2010: 5), and civil wars not only have 'adverse consequences for development,' but also are 'a failure of development' (World Bank 2003: ix, emphasis in original). During civil wars, countries' economic growth slows down by about 2.2% when compared to peace time (Collier 1999). Therefore, the World Bank (2003: 13) report refers to civil wars as 'development in reverse.'

By responding to political instability and violence, providing property rights and enforceable contracts, and tackling corruption, fragile countries can escape the 'fragility trap' and enjoy sustained economic growth (Andrimihaja et al. 2011). Violence and fear of violence have important economic costs for societies, because violence generates 'costs in the form of property damage, physical injury or psychological trauma' and fear of violence changes 'investment and consumption patterns' (IEP 2020: 42). The economic costs of 'preventing and dealing with the consequences of violence divert public and private resources away from productive activities,' and are divided into three categories: 'direct costs, indirect costs, and a multiplier effect' (IEP 2020: 42). The direct costs have 'immediate consequences on the victims, perpetrators, and public systems including health, judicial and public safety' (IEP 2020: 42). The indirect cost of violence includes longer-term costs, such as 'lost productivity, psychological effects and the impact of violence on the perception of safety and security in society' (IEP 2020: 42). The multiplier effect 'represents the economic benefits that would be generated by the diversion of expenditure away from sunk costs … into more productive alternatives that would better improve the economy' (IEP 2020: 42). The direct and indirect costs of violence effectively illustrate the importance of violence-prevention in enhancing economic welfare.

Therefore, many scholars argue that development may be seen as a 'means to reduce violence and enhance peace and stability' (Bergenas and Mahoney 2016; Collinson et al. 2010: 5; Zoellick 2008). They note that 'active support from security and defense players may actually improve the sustainability of development operations in fragile and failing states, which saw a 9.3 percent drop in allocated [Official Development Assistance] ODA since 2013' (Bergenas & Mahoney 2016). This is referred to as 'securing development' in terms of 'simultaneity rather than sequencing' by Zoellick (2008: 5), who argues that both development and security communities should recognize the importance of addressing security and development challenges simultaneously. A good example to this model is the Provincial Reconstruction Teams (PRTs) in Iraq and Afghanistan (Zoellick 2008).

Some scholars argue that much progress has been made to merge the development and security policies and to create an inclusive, organic, and transparent network (Duffield 2001: 35–36). Others note that there is room for improvement and recommend having 'more interaction on the ground between security and development staff' in order to enable better communication on 'their respective interests, capabilities, and limitations' (Zoellick 2008: 5). While many point out the synergy between security/peace and development, there are some that draw attention to potential hazards. For instance, development aid may increase 'the risks of atrocity crimes' (SDG-16 Conference 2019: 12). The leading experts therefore call for the development and security actors to keep their obligation to 'do no harm' (SDG-16 Conference 2019: 12).

Critical scholars like Duffield (2007) draw attention to 'securitising development' (Quoted in Collinson et al. 2010: 5). They highlight the 'continuing tension' between development and security circles, where the former 'remains highly diffident, defensive and sometimes openly hostile to much of what may be seen as falling under the banner of stabilisation,' due to anxieties about 'the goals of humanitarian action' (Collinson et al. 2010: 4). They note that the simultaneous conduct of development assistance and counterterrorism operations may lead to confusion about the objectives of the development missions. This is especially the case when 'military troops become actively engaged in humanitarian or development assistance activities,' leading to difficulty in the eyes of the local populations 'to separate the aid community from fighting forces' (Schnabel & Farr: 2012: 13).

On a related point, some experts point to the politicization of the relationship between security and development during the Cold War (Duffield 2001) and the War on Terror (Wulf 2011). For instance, in the aftermath of the 9/11 terrorist attacks, the George W. Bush Administration's first *National Security Strategy* focused on the failed states. Failed states often serve as 'safe havens and staging grounds for terrorist organizations,' undermine regional stability with 'significant economic and security costs to neighboring states,' and create refugee flows, trafficking, and lost trade and investment opportunities (Rice 2003). This has created a more security-centered approach towards failed states, rather than a more development-centered approach.

Accordingly, many are alarmed by the military 'increasingly aiming to co-opt the NGO community under a discourse based on the need to break cultural barriers and misunderstandings, and the assumption of sharing common goals' (Ferreiro 2012). They contend that increased linkages between security and development are 'an attempt to subordinate help to poor people to the short-term security concerns of Western nation states and their elites' (Bueger & Vennesson 2009: 4). They add that 'military relief operations within counter-insurgency (COIN) strategies and the mushrooming of militarized contractors have contributed to greater confusion' (Ferreiro 2012). Others emphasize the challenges of coordinating development and security policies and addressing the 'root causes' of fragility and conflict (Bueger & Vennesson 2009). Their criticism is that security and development are 'extremely broad and elusive concepts' (Bueger & Vennesson 2009; Tschirgi 2005: 4).

Many analysts caution against short-term relief action hurting 'long-term capacity development' (Blind 2019: 3; Schnabel & Farr 2012; Wolff & Dursun-Özkanca 2012). Others argue that security and development concerns have rarely been linked in an institutional framework and attract attention to the existence of 'rigidly divided disciplinary approaches and organisational structures' that do not meet 'people's needs on the ground' (Krause & Jütersonke 2005; Schnabel & Farr 2012: 12). They give the example of the 'unevenness' with which the UN Development Programme (UNDP) 'applies a conflict-sensitive lens to its development interventions, even when these take place in fragile, conflict and post-conflict settings' (Schnabel & Farr 2012: 12). Such critics note that even though development and security/peace activities pursue similar goals, they 'invest little effort in learning from each other's experience,' and applying it in their own activities (Schnabel & Farr 2012: 15). Against this background, it is important to note that *Agenda 2030* and the SDGs are an attempt to respond to such criticisms, as they link peace and security as well as development concerns in an institutional framework. Having established the dynamics between security and development, this manuscript next provides an overview of the literature on SSG/R, *Agenda 2030*, and SDG-16.

CHAPTER 2

Literature Review

a. The literature on SSG/R

SSR is a relatively novel and evolving concept that originally emerged out of scholarship on civil-military relations (CMR) (Bruneau & Matei 2008; Chuter 2006; Crossley-Frolick & Dursun-Özkanca 2012; Edmunds 2007). As noted above, it was first coined by Short (Sedra 2010), who first proposed that security and sustainable development are inextricably linked (Dursun-Özkanca & Vandemoortele 2012). SSR and SSG have received increasing recognition for their contributions to effective democratization, good governance, sustaining peace, conflict prevention, and post-conflict reconstruction since the end of the 1990s (Hänggi 2003; OECD 2008; Dursun-Özkanca 2014; UN Peacekeeping 2020). The security sector is defined by the OECD-DAC as:

> core security actors (e.g. armed forces, police, gendarmerie, border guards, customs and immigration, and intelligence and security services); security management and oversight bodies (e.g. ministries of defense and internal affairs, financial management bodies and public complaints commissions); justice and law enforcement institutions (e.g. the judiciary, prisons, prosecution services, traditional justice systems); and non-statutory security forces (e.g. private security companies, guerrilla armies and private militia) (OECD 2005: 5).

The UN defines SSR as:

> a process of assessment, review and implementation as well as monitoring and evaluation led by national authorities that has as its goal the enhancement of effective and accountable security for the State and its peoples without discrimination and with full respect for human rights and the rule of law (UN Department of Peacekeeping Operations 2012: 2).

How to cite this book chapter:
Dursun-Özkanca, O. 2021. *The Nexus Between Security Sector Governance/Reform and Sustainable Development Goal-16: An Examination of Conceptual Linkages and Policy Recommendations.* Pp. 11–19. London: Ubiquity Press. DOI: https://doi.org/10.5334/bcm.b. License: CC-BY-NC

SSG is the application of the principles of good governance, such as accountability, transparency, rule of law, participation, responsiveness, effectiveness, and efficiency to a state's security sector (The Geneva Centre for the Democratic Control of Armed Forces [DCAF] 2015). It involves both 'the formal and informal influences of all the structures, institutions and actors involved in provision, management and oversight of security and justice at national and local levels' (Myrttinen 2019: 13). It sees justice and security as public goods and hence calls for the establishment of 'transparent policies and practices' that are 'within a framework for democratic governance that respects human rights and the rule of law' (Myrttinen 2019: 13). In that sense, it not only involves the formal actors, but also includes informal and non-state actors in security provision and oversight.

Good SSG should be regarded as 'the goal,' whereas 'SSR, or security sector transformation, is a way of getting there' (Myrttinen 2019: 14). In other words, if there are problems with the administration of SSG in a particular country in a way that its security sector 'is not inclusive, is partial and corrupt, unresponsive, incoherent, ineffective and inefficient and/or unaccountable to the public,' that country's security sector is in need of reform (Schnabel 2012: 53). SSR is 'often targeted at specific parts of the justice and security sector, e.g. police reform, justice reform or penal reform' (Myrttinen 2019: 14). As noted by OECD-DAC (2007: 10), SSR aims at:

> i) the improvement of basic security and justice service delivery, ii) the establishment of an effective governance, oversight and accountability system; and iii) the development of local leadership and ownership of a reform process to review the capacity and technical needs of the security system.

SSG emphasizes that there should be clear guidelines for security provision along with independent oversight to ensure that these guidelines are properly implemented by the authorities. It further highlights the availability of information to those who are affected by decisions on the security sector and their implementation. Rule of law has a central place in SSG, as the expectation is that all the laws are enforced consistently, impartially, and in line with the international and national human rights laws and norms. Inclusivity is similarly important for SSG, meaning that 'all men and women of all backgrounds have the opportunity to participate in decision-making and service provision on a free, equitable and inclusive basis, either directly or through legitimate representative institutions' (DCAF 2015: 3). SSG also places high importance on responsiveness to ensure that security and justice institutions are sensitive to the needs of the whole of the population and 'perform their missions in the spirit of a culture of service' (DCAF 2015: 3). Finally, effectiveness and efficiency are important in SSG, so that the institutions fulfill their responsibilities within the bounds of high professional standards and 'make the best possible use of public resources' when fulfilling their responsibilities (DCAF 2015: 3).

Since the 1990s, SSG principles have been disseminated by a variety of organizations, such as the UN, the Organization for Security and Co-operation in Europe (OSCE), the OECD-DAC, the EU, and the African Union (AU) (DCAF 2015). Similarly, the UN Secretary-General's reports on SSR dated 2008 and 2013 'endorsed the principles of good SSG' (DCAF 2015: 8). In the aftermath of the Cold War, numerous factors brought about the development and evolution of the SSG/R literature. Such factors include concerns of donor countries about how conflicts hinder sustainable development in the developing parts of the world (Brzoska 2000; Hendrickson & Karkoszka 2002; Law & Myshlovska 2008), the rechanneling of defense/security-related financial resources to development projects (Brzoska 2000, 2003; Hänggi 2009), and a novel emphasis on governance, transparency, accountability, and democratic CMR in countries that were undergoing political transitions, especially from authoritarian to democratic regimes, in Central and Eastern Europe (Brzoska 2000; Chanaa 2002; Hänggi 2009). Also included among these factors are Western governments' desire to promote good governance and reform the military, police, border guards, and judicial institutions (Brzoska 2000; Chanaa 2002; Hänggi 2009), a new understanding of security in the form of the concept of human security (Ball and Hendrickson 2009; Doelle & de Harven 2008; Hänggi 2003; Sedra 2006a, 2006b), a surge of the importance of peacebuilding in post-conflict settings (Brzoska 2000; Hänggi 2009; Law & Myshlovska 2008), and an emphasis on transitional justice in post-conflict settings (Crossley-Frolick & Dursun-Özkanca 2012; Dursun-Özkanca & Crossley-Frolick 2012). More recently, the SSG principles and SSR have become even more important against the background of 'a growing trend towards authoritarianism, as institutions, including the judiciary, become less independent and less able to constrain government powers' (The 2019 World Justice Project Rule of Law Index, quoted in the Global Alliance 2019: 114). In its Resolution 2553 passed in early December 2020, the UNSC reiterated its commitment to SSG/R as well as *Agenda 2030* (UNSC 2020b).

There is a multitude of works in the SSG/R literature that examine the role played by external actors in conducting SSR (Bryden 2007; Caparini 2003; Dursun-Özkanca 2014; Spence & Fluri 2008; Tadesse 2010; Vetschera and Damian 2006). In 2014, UNSC Resolution 2151 reemphasized the importance of the national or local ownership concept in SSR and encouraged states to incorporate 'an inclusive national vision,' based on the local population's needs. The resolution also called for better integration of SSR into broader national political processes, and emphasized the centrality of monitoring and evaluation SSR, and 'strengthening support to sector-wide initiatives that enhance the governance and performance of the security sector' (UN Peacekeeping 2020). Nonetheless, the challenge of ensuring local ownership remains in SSR implementation, and there is disagreement in the literature over the connection between SSG/R, local ownership, and statebuilding, and 'whether international administrations represent an imperial enterprise or are a welcome form of providing governance for states emerging from conflict' (Peter 2013: 435). Which and what kind of local actors to involve, when to make the transition to local ownership, and the logistics/resources through which ownership is practiced all emerge as key items in the local ownership agenda (Caplan 2006; Chesterman 2007; Dursun-Özkanca 2018; Dursun-Özkanca & Vandemoortele 2012; Narten 2008). When SSR has 'political traction and national ownership,' it helps to facilitate establishing rule of law, to fight against impunity, and to restore 'the social contract on which stability depends' (UN Peacekeeping 2020). Therefore, the current manuscript allocates special attention to the concept of local ownership as it relates to the linkages between SSG/R and SDG-16. It also sheds light on the interconnections between SSG/R and SDG-16 in terms of oversight and accountability.

i. SSG/R and development

SSR has hybrid origins going back to both security and development literatures. It is a 'highly intersectional concept' that relies on 'effective collaboration and linking of security and development needs assessments, conducted and implemented by actors from both communities' (Schnabel 2012: 55). It has roots in the development donor debate on how to more effectively target and implement development assistance in security-related fields (Baldassini et al. 2018; Brzoska 2003). In this context, it is important to talk about political conditionality, because democratic principles, human rights, and good governance are typically presented 'as a condition for economic assistance' (Wulf 2011: 353). Therefore, the debates on SSG/R frequently mirror the discussions provided in the security-development nexus section above.

SSR and development reinforce each other. It serves to advance both human security and human development (Schnabel & Farr 2012). In his 2008 report on SSR, then UN Secretary-General Ban Ki-moon criticized the UN's involvement in SSR as piecemeal and lacking a common framework and a coherent system-wide approach and called for a 'holistic and coherent United Nations approach' to SSR in order to 'provide a basis for a transparent framework for reform and international principles consistent with the Charter of the United Nations and human rights laws and standards' (UNSG 2008: 2). He added that the provision of assistance on SSR would also 'increase the effectiveness and efficiency' of the UN peacekeeping operations, 'facilitating early recovery from conflict and helping to build the conditions necessary for sustainable peace and development' (UNSG 2008: 2).

The legitimacy and effectiveness of SSR missions have important repercussions on fragile states' capability to build and pay for their 'own reliable police and armed forces' (Zoellick 2008: 6). While 'Properly organized and trained, local police and military are key to securing public support, gaining intelligence, and sustaining security,' 'ill-trained forces' that undermine the government's legitimacy run the risk of perpetuating or making an already-destructive situation worse (Zoellick 2008: 6). Consequently, effective SSR and disarmament, demobilization, and reintegration (DDR) through 'job training and placement for ex-combatants' are critical for peacebuilding (Zoellick 2008: 6). This emphasizes the significance of the security-development nexus in SSR.

SSR and development communities share common goals, including a commitment to peace and justice 'via consultative and bottom-up programme planning' (Winkler 2012: vii). Consequently, 'short-cutting SSR, particularly by failing to take the governance dimensions seriously and pursuing SSR in isolation from larger development and governance reform priorities' may lead to further instability (Schnabel & Farr 2012: 12). SSR missions should be informed by SSG. Otherwise, in the long run, they 'may turn out to be counterproductive not just to SSR aims, but to development and peace-building objectives as well' (Schnabel & Farr 2012: 12–13). Accordingly, there are calls for a more systematic collection of empirical evidence to demonstrate how SSR and development 'inter-operate' (Farr, Schnabel & Krupanski 2012: 336).

Additionally, many note an enduring prejudice in the donor community against working with security sector players, especially the military (Brzoska 2003). On this topic, Farr, Schnabel and Krupanski (2012: 327) ask the development community 'to step up and assume responsibility, leadership and ownership,' adding that 'It does not serve anyone to remain passive and simply criticise.' They conclude, 'Stove-piping of assistance missions between security and development communities is counterproductive to sustainable reforms, change, stability and poverty reduction' (Farr, Schnabel & Krupanski 2012: 327).

Others recommend that SSR be 'implemented as a companion to development assistance' 'as a long-term project, designed in a participatory and inclusive manner in collaboration with state and non-state actors,' with a focus on local ownership and good governance and warn that half-hearted SSR activities that fall short of these criteria 'will do more harm than good' (Schnabel 2012: 54). For instance, in 2014, UNSC 2151 emphasized the importance of SSG/R and reassured that member states are 'committed to improving the contributions and relevance of security sector reform to the wider development agenda' (UN Peacekeeping 2020). SSR and SSG are both 'preventive' measures as well as 'long-term development' goals (UN Peacekeeping 2020). Illustrating the linkages between security and development, the UN utilizes SSR not only in its peace operations, but also in 'non-mission settings, in response to national requests, and in transition settings, where peace operations are withdrawing but where ongoing security sector assistance is needed' (UN Peacekeeping 2020).

In post-conflict societies, SSR 'is a determining factor for the exit of a peacekeeping operation, early recovery, sustainable peacebuilding and longer-term development,' and 'is a sine qua non for sustainable economic and political development' (UN Peacekeeping 2020). For instance, if police reform, a common component of SSR, is effectively administered, it will curb corruption and inefficiencies in the police force, leading to more criminals being brought to justice (Dursun-Özkanca & Vandemoortele 2012). If justice reform, another common component of SSR, has not been reformed properly, those criminals may escape justice by bribing their way out (Larivé 2012). Therefore, it is important to engage in 'a holistic, comprehensive and broadly defined approach that includes many if not all security-providing institutions in the society' (Dursun-Özkanca & Vandemoortele 2012; Schnabel & Farr: 2012: 13).

SSR circles have learned lessons from both development and security communities and the practitioners of SSR increasingly acknowledge that the security sector should be addressed as a whole (Faleg 2012). Even then, greater synergy between SSR and development activities through a deeper emphasis on mutual planning, design, implementation, monitoring, and assessment of these activities may 'enhance each other's positive impact on society' (Schnabel & Farr 2012: 11). Much lip service has been paid to this synergy on paper, nevertheless, there have been significant gaps in the implementation of these ideals (Schnabel & Farr 2012; Wolff & Dursun-Özkanca 2012).

ii. Critiques of the SSR-development nexus

The literature on SSG/R recognizes that each security sector is interlinked at least in principle, 'but remains lacking in its practical implementation' (Dursun-Özkanca & Vandemoortele 2012: 151). As warned by a recent study, if SSR's 'development roots' are not recognized, 'the supposed responsibility and professed enthusiasm of the SSR/G community towards upholding and serving broader development goals through SSR remain ambivalent at best' (Baldassini et al. 2018: 43). Mirroring the discussions explained in the previous section, others attract attention to the risk of securitization in SSR (Buzan 2007; Schnabel & Farr 2012; Short 2014; Wulf 2011). They warn that when 'armed forces simultaneously wage a military campaign and train local military or police,' the important principles of SSR, such as civilian oversight or democratic governance may 'get lost' (Schnabel & Farr 2012: 13). Many experts emphasize the primacy of national interests in SSR missions (Justaert 2012), which indicate a favoring of the security aspect over development. Clare Short, the former UK Secretary of State for International Development, who first coined the term SSR in 1998 (Sedra 2010), warned that the SSR 'concept might be deployed as a cover for interventions that focus less on the needs of local people and more on Western security interests' (Short 2014: ix).

Moreover, there are heated debates about the need for long-term and 'sustainable' SSR approaches to deliver the desired outcomes (Schnabel & Farr 2012: 16). Many highlight that long-term approaches 'do not always gain the respect and support of short-sighted external actors' who prefer a 'highly technical approach' that seeks 'to replicate templates and blueprints that have worked for them at home' (Schnabel and Farr 2012: 16). As Wolff and Dursun-Özkanca (2012: 309) note, the fact that the 'regional and international organisations do not often fail in their [self-assigned] conflict management efforts' is 'partly due to a more realistic and cautious definition of mission mandates,' which seek more 'limited' and 'vaguely-defined goals,' instead of 'peace.' Consequently, a more comprehensive security approach, 'spanning a breadth of themes and actors when it comes to defining what security means and for whom, who should be involved in providing security and what role security plays for human development and vice versa,' emerges as a central theme in SSR-development nexus (Baldassini et al. 2018: 38–39).

Other scholars further point out the dangers of institution building during an ongoing civil war or famine, by citing that corruption, war, and famine 'fuel each other' and 'compound economic distress and strife' (Athorpe 1997; Gaile & Ferguson 1996, quoted in Blind 2019). They note, 'Defaulting on comprehensive SSR in favour of quick-fix, politically opportunist approaches to do 'something' with 'someone' will not win the trust of either the development or the security community' (Baldassini et al. 2018: 39). Others like Wulf (2011: 342) identify a central dilemma in the SSR-development nexus, by posing the question: 'Will SSR lead to a democratisation of the security sector and thus contribute to development, or will development assistance be manipulated to function as a military "force multiplier"?' They warn, 'If the causes of insecurity are misperceived, then programmes or suggested remedies might be inefficient or even counterproductive' (Wulf 2011: 353). Next, this manuscript delves into an overview of the literature on sustainable development, *Agenda 2030*, and SDG-16.

b. The literature on sustainable development, *Agenda 2030*, and SDG-16

The sustainable development concept is derived from the Malthusian theory, which postulates that 'human population tended to grow in a geometric progression, while subsistence could grow in only an arithmetic progression, and for that matter, population growth was likely to outstrip the capacity of the natural resources to support the needs of the increasing population' (Mensah & Casadevall 2019: 6–7). It argues that if left unchecked, the population growth rate will deplete humans of natural resources (Mensah & Casadevall 2019).

The origin of the modern concept of sustainable development goes back to 1983, to the foundation of the World Commission on Environment and Development (WCED). The Commission's mandate was to 'formulate realistic proposals' for dealing with environment and development issues, 'to propose new forms of international cooperation' on such issues, and 'to raise the levels of understanding and commitment to action of individuals, voluntary organizations, businesses, institutes, and governments' (WCED 1987: 12). As stated in the WCED report, *Our Common Future* (also known as *the Brundtland Report*), which directly referred to the sustainable development concept for the first time, 'Humanity has the ability to make development sustainable to ensure that it meets the needs of the present without compromising the ability of future generations to meet their own needs' (WCED 1987: 15).

The concept of human development was 'pioneered' by Mahbub ul Haq, under UNDP's leadership, and 'helped to shift the focus of development attention away from an overarching concentration on the growth of inanimate objects of convenience, such as commodities produced... to the quality and richness of human lives' (The Commission on Human Security 2003: 8). Human development aims at 'removing the various hindrances that restrain and restrict human lives and prevent its blossoming' (The Commission on Human Security 2003: 8). Human development literature tends 'to concentrate on "growth with equity"' (The Commission on Human Security 2003: 8). Over time, the concept of development was deepened by underlining the importance of human security (Bueger & Vennesson 2009).

i. Millennium Development Goals (MDGs)

The *Our Common Future* report was followed by the UN Conference on the Environment and Development (UNCED), also known as the Rio Earth Summit of 1992, the largest international gathering at the beginning of the 1990s (Paul 2008; Mensah & Casadevall 2019). Three years later, the international community negotiated the Kyoto Protocol (Paul 2008; Mensah & Casadevall 2019). In 2000, the Millennium Summit was held in New York City, launching the eight MDGs (Paul 2008; Mensah & Casadevall 2019), which included: 1) eradicate extreme poverty and hunger, 2) achieve universal primary education, 3) promote gender equality and empower women, 4) reduce child mortality, 5) improve maternal health, 6) combat HIV/AIDS, malaria, and other diseases, 7) ensure environmental sustainability, and 8) develop a global partnership for development (*UN Millennium Declaration* 2000).

As put by the *UN Millennium Project* (2005: 1), MDGs were 'time-bound and quantified targets' to address 'extreme poverty' and its various dimensions, such as 'income poverty, hunger, disease, lack of adequate shelter, and exclusion,' and to promote 'gender equality, education, and environmental sustainability.' They are also 'basic human rights' as pledged in the Universal Declaration of Human Rights and the UN Millennium Declaration (*UN Millennium Project* 2005: 1). They achieved some important outcomes, especially with regards to the anti-poverty movement (UN 2015). As then UN Secretary-General Ban Ki-moon noted in the Foreword of the last *Millennium Development Goals Report* in 2015 (UN 2015: 3), 'The MDGs helped to lift more than one billion people out of extreme poverty, to make inroads against hunger, to enable more girls to attend school than ever before and to protect our planet.' They also created 'innovative partnerships, galvanized public opinion and showed the immense value of setting ambitious goals' (UN 2015: 3). They put 'people and their immediate needs at the forefront' of 'decision-making in developed and developing countries alike' (UN 2015: 3).

Nevertheless, as acknowledged by Ban Ki-moon (UN 2015: 3), 'inequalities persist and … progress has been uneven,' as most of the world's extremely poor people live in five countries, problems with women's health continue, and disparities between urban and rural areas 'remain pronounced' (UN 2015: 3). The final *Millennium Development Goals Report* in 2015 emphasized that 'conflicts remain the biggest threat to human development' (UN 2015: 8). Therefore, the track record of the MDGs has been 'uneven across regions and countries, leaving significant gaps,' and '[m]illions of people are being left behind, especially the poorest and those disadvantaged because of their sex, age, disability, ethnicity or geographic location' (UN 2015: 8).

Some in the literature criticized the assessment of the MDGs, claiming that the focus on the negatives created a hurdle for further progress. To illustrate, Easterly (2009: 26) noted, 'The statement that "Africa will miss all the MDGs" … has the unfortunate effect of making African successes look like failures.' Others emphasized the missing goal of reduction of inequalities between the Global North and Global South (Fukuda-Parr 2010) and omitted focus on the poorest parts of the Global South due to the use of national averages and aggregated data (Brikci & Holder 2011). Yet others criticized the MDGs for their lack of focus on human rights and security (Fehling et al. 2013; Hill et al. 2010; Waage et al. 2010; Ziai 2011). Finally, the MDGs received criticism for being 'addressed in isolation' from one another and for the lack of 'an inclusive consultation process' during their formulation (International Institute for Sustainable Development [IISD] 2016). The lack of a consultative process is said to have contributed to 'a lack of understanding of the Goals and their targets at the national level during the initial implementation stage' (IISD 2016).

ii. The Sustainable Development Goals (SDGs)

The SDG process was initiated at the 2006 UN General Assembly, under the leadership of South African President Mbeki calling for the execution of the Johannesburg Plan of Implementation adopted in 2002 (Dodds & Bartram 2016; Tosun & Leininger 2017). In 2012, the UN Conference on Sustainable Development (UNCSD), also known as Rio+ 20 was held, focusing on making sustainable development a key agenda item for the UN and the development of new SDGs beginning in 2015 (Weitz et al. 2017). In 2015, the UN adopted its *Agenda 2030,* containing 17 SDGs, and called member states to action 'to end poverty, protect the planet and improve the lives and prospects of everyone, everywhere' by 2030 (UN General Assembly 2015). It incorporated five Ps: 'people, planet, prosperity, peace and partnerships' (Guo 2017; Hylton 2019; Mensah & Casadevall 2019; Zhai & Chang 2019). At the UN Sustainable Development Summit in 2015, 'a global process of social and political adaptation to limits posed by the natural resource base' was initiated (Tosun & Leininger 2017: 1). UN's *Agenda 2030* pledged 'enhanced capacity-building support for developing countries, including the strengthening of national data systems and evaluation programmes, particularly in African countries, least developed countries, small island developing States, landlocked developing countries and middle-income countries' (UNGA 2015: 32). Collection of systematic data at the national level will help better achieve the targets of SDG-16 (DCAF, OSCE/ODIHR and UN Women 2019: 9). But here, a major negative factor is that some states 'shy away from collecting data that may be embarrassing, such as data related to corruption and bribery' (Hope 2020b: 73).

Following the MDGs, the SDGs are 17 goals, which represented 'a break with the traditional global approach to spurring sustainable development (which was, *inter alia*, based on the negotiation of intergovernmental agreements that largely promoted a "work in silos" approach)' (IISD 2016). Furthermore, the process of constructing the national SDG plans was also drastically different than the process during the MDGs (IISD 2016). The SDGs, unlike their predecessor MDGs, were able to incorporate feedback from a variety of constituencies and sought to deepen the collaboration with various stakeholders.

As noted in the *UNDP Support for the Implementation of Sustainable Development Goal-16* (UNDP 2016: 4) document, 'Lessons learned from the implementation of the MDGs show that progress towards achieving the MDGs was often hampered by conflict, a lack of rule of law and weak institutions.' As the Report of the Secretary-General (UNSG 2013: 6) acknowledges, 'While in the Millennium Declaration of 2000 states recognized the importance of peacebuilding and citizen security, those concerns were not adequately reflected in the Millennium Development Goals.' Hence, the specific goals and targets of the MDGs 'did not incorporate key security, human rights and rule of law factors that form the basis for development' (UNSG 2013: 6). Accordingly, there were 'calls for an increased focus on security in defining the post-Millennium Development Goal agenda,' which were addressed through the dialogue via the Global Thematic Consultation on Conflict, Violence and Disaster from July 2012 to March 2013 (UNSG 2013: 6).

The international community drew important lessons from the MDGs, especially when it comes to acknowledging the significance of governance as an explanatory factor for the uneven track record of countries on the MDGs (The Global Alliance 2019). The SDGs are universal, integrated, and indivisible (Tosun & Leininger 2017; UNGA 2015; Weitz et al. 2017). Unlike the MDGs, there are many intersectoral SDGs that reinforce each other (Nilsson et al. 2016). For instance, SDG-10 and SDG-16 are generally regarded as prerequisites for accomplishing other SDGs (Tosun & Leininger 2017). SDG-16 is particularly identified as an 'enabler' of other goals by many (SDG-16 Conference 2019; Tosun & Leininger 2017: 5). SDG-10 and SDG-16 'serve to guide investments in human capital development, poverty eradication, inequality reduction and boosting inclusion, thus helping reduce bases for conflict' (SDG-16 Conference 2019: 2) and 'serve as catalysts for achieving many other SDG targets' (SDG-16 Conference 2019: 6).

'Policy integration' is an important pre-condition for successful implementation of *Agenda 2030* (Tosun & Leininger 2017: 10). Therefore, many studies put emphasis on the monitoring, assessment, implementation, and governance innovation of the SDGs (Allen et al. 2018; Kanie & Biermann 2017; Mensah and Casadevall 2019; Tosun & Leininger 2017). There is the Mainstreaming, Acceleration and Policy Support (MAPS) process that the UN uses to help member states integrate the SDGs into their national development processes (The Global Alliance 2019). In that context, there is a key partnership, titled 'The New Deal' between G7+ countries and OECD-DAC donors that was established in 2011. It 'recognizes the nexus between peace and development and guides the effective engagement of actors in conflict-affected countries' through 'peacebuilding and statebuilding goals,' such as 'inclusive and legitimate politics, security and justice, economic foundation and revenue and services' (The Global Alliance 2019: 48). It highlights 'the importance of addressing the underlying causes of conflict' (UNSG 2013: 6). Finally, the High-Level Political Forum on Sustainable Development (HLPF), which is the main UN platform on sustainable development, has a vital role in the 'follow-up and review' of the *2030 Agenda* and the SDGs, especially at the global level (UN General Assembly 2016).

On the assessment and furthering of SDG-16, there is a coordination platform called the Global Alliance for Reporting Progress on Peaceful, Just and Inclusive Societies (also known as the SDG-16 Alliance or the Global Alliance). It coordinates action on the part of the UN Member

States, the private sector, and civil society organizations (CSOs) to advance the goal of establishing peace, justice, and strong institutions. It functions as 'the international system's only multi-stakeholder platform for joint decision-making and action at the global and national level,' emphasizing 'evidence-based and multi-stakeholder action' (The Global Alliance 2020). For instance, it publishes the SDG16+ reports globally, and aims at accelerating progress on SDG-16 targets. The term 'SDG-16+,' is 'coined to reflect the linkages between goals and targets beyond SDG-16 that embody commitments to peace, justice, and inclusion across all the SDGs' (The Global Alliance 2019: 18). It attracts attention to the interdependence between SDG-16 and 'the 24 other targets of other SDGs that directly measure an aspect of peace, justice and inclusion' (The Global Alliance 2019: 18).

Besides the Global Alliance, other cross-country initiatives providing technical support to UN member states and civil society organizations on the implementation of SDGs across peace, justice, and inclusion include the Transparency, Accountability and Participation (TAP) Network, Pathfinders for Peaceful, Just and Inclusive Societies, 16 Plus Forum, the Effective Institutions Platform (EIP), the Sustainable Development Goals Fund (SDGF), the Partnership Against Corruption Initiative (PACI), SDG-16 Data Initiative and the Open Government Partnership (OGP), and the European Fund for Sustainable Development (EFSD) (The Global Alliance 2019). Many engage in public-private partnerships (PPPs) to support SDG-16+.

CHAPTER 3

SDG-16: Content and Controversies

a. SDG-16 content

As noted earlier, security and development spheres have only been brought together concretely recently under the institutional framework of the SDGs. Prior to the SDGs, development actors did not show much interest in security affairs and security circles did not sufficiently emphasize development. Furthermore, the security-development nexus section already discussed the enduring skepticism between the development and security circles against each other.

The SDGs in general, and SDG-16 in particular, incorporate both development- and peace/security-related targets. SDG-16 emphasizes peacebuilding, good governance, and sustainable development. It sets the goal of promoting just, peaceful, and inclusive societies. It specifically focuses on ending violence, promoting the rule of law, strengthening institutions, and increasing access to justice through responsive and representative decision making and transparency (UN 2020a). In that sense, it contains elements that emphasize negative peace as well as positive peace (Radović 2019). To illustrate, it targets negative peace measures, such as physical violence and homicide rates, as well as positive peace measures, such as combating corruption, establishing the rule of law, transparency, accountability, and responsive, inclusive, participatory, and representative decision making.

SDG-16 is arguably the most ambitious among all 17 SDGs and will have a multiplier effect on other SDGs, as its mandate crosscuts the mandates of many other SDGs. In words of a recent study, 'SDG-16 represents an unprecedented opportunity to launch a new era of pragmatic action that simultaneously works toward making poverty history, while mitigating the negative consequences from conflict and insecurity' (Bergenas & Mahoney 2016). As noted by UNGA (2015: 25–26), SDG-16 contains the 12 targets listed in Table 1.

How to cite this book chapter:
Dursun-Özkanca, O. 2021. *The Nexus Between Security Sector Governance/Reform and Sustainable Development Goal-16: An Examination of Conceptual Linkages and Policy Recommendations.* Pp. 21–25. London: Ubiquity Press. DOI: https://doi.org/10.5334/bcm.c. License: CC-BY-NC

Table 1: SDG-16 Targets.

16.1 Significantly reduce all forms of violence and related death rates everywhere
16.2 End abuse, exploitation, trafficking, and all forms of violence against and torture of children
16.3 Promote the rule of law at the national and international levels and ensure equal access to justice for all
16.4 By 2030, significantly reduce illicit financial and arms flows, strengthen the recovery and return of stolen assets and combat all forms of organized crime
16.5 Substantially reduce corruption and bribery in all their forms
16.6 Develop effective, accountable, and transparent institutions at all levels
16.7 Ensure responsive, inclusive, participatory, and representative decision making at all levels
16.8 Broaden and strengthen the participation of developing countries in the institutions of global governance
16.9 By 2030, provide legal identity for all, including birth registration
16.10 Ensure public access to information and protect fundamental freedoms, in accordance with national legislation and international agreements
16.a Strengthen relevant national institutions, including through international cooperation, for building capacity at all levels, in particular in developing countries, to prevent violence and combat terrorism and crime
16.b Promote and enforce non-discriminatory laws and policies for sustainable development

Source: UNGA (2015: 25–26).

Targets 16.a and 16.b are what are referred to as the Means of Implementation (MOI) Targets, which are included for all 17 SDG targets. They 'draw specific attention to the enabling actions that underpin the achievement of the core SDG Targets and should be read in conjunction with SDG-17,' which seeks to boost the means of implementation and reinvigorate the global partnership for sustainable development (TAP Network 2016: 11). The above list of goals effectively illustrates the sentiment that is aptly summarized by the Global Alliance (2019: 20):

> Without sustained peace, which goes beyond the mere absence of violence and includes respect for human rights and the rule of law, development gains are reversed. And without inclusion and access to justice for all, inequalities in poverty reduction and socio-economic development will increase and countries' commitments to leaving no one behind will not be met.

While it is undoubtedly commendable that SDG-16 seeks to link security and development together, the path towards the adoption of SDG-16 has not been without challenges and controversies. Next, this manuscript provides a brief summary of the debates that revolved around SDG-16 in linking the spheres of development and security together. Here, it is especially important to unpack the criticisms coming from the development circles.

b. SDG-16 controversies

Many in the development community warned about the potential dangers of linking the spheres of development and security together under SDG-16. They noted that this tendency is 'alarming' (Möller-Loswick 2017) and critics claimed that the international community is 'securitizing development' (Buzan 2007; Duffield 2001; Lazarus 2020: 166; Möller-Loswick 2017). First and foremost, security and development circles have been circumspect about working closely with each other, 'due to uncertainty about the impact ... it has on their preparedness and capacity to address their core business' (Baldassini et al. 2018: 23). For instance, Lazarus (2020) voices skepticism about the motivations behind SDG-16 and concludes, 'What we see in SDG-16 is a goal of empowerment, but the licence it gives to the idea of crime control and the coercion of private violence isn't always about empowerment. It is also about social control' (Lazarus 2020: 168). Möller-Loswick (2017) adds that 'peace goal could put the wider development agenda at risk,' as some international actors pursue 'SDG16 to justify "securitised" and counter-produc- tive approaches to development,' by adopting 'reactive, securitised and poorly thought-through responses to security threats.' Besides 'securitization,' there are also concerns about 'militariza- tion' or 'misuse' of development assistance 'for military purposes' (Schnabel & Farr 2012; Wulf 2011: 342). As Wulf (2011: 342) notes, failed and failing states, post-conflict reconstruction, and the War on Terror 'have given rise to efforts to use development assistance for military and stra- tegic purposes' (Wulf 2011: 342).

Moreover, there are fears of 'takeover by one agenda and one set of actors' in the field. The con- cern is that the cooperation between development and security circles 'in the design and imple- mentation of joint projects' may lead to one group being dominated or undermined by the other using the excuse of 'expediency and efficiency' of the operation to 'skew the nature of the joint activity' (Baldassini et al. 2018: 24). Here, development circles are concerned that the security circles 'will dominate and possibly take over' due to their 'more rigorous structure and culture, financial capacities, access and territorial reach' (Baldassini et al. 2018: 24).

Additionally, more eyebrows were raised in the development community as a result of the changes made into the OECD-DAC ODA rules. In 2012, the OECD decided to modernize the ODA concept to more accurately reflect development activities in the official data. Given the high costs of meeting the goals of sustainable development mentioned at Rio+ 20, some donors wanted to incentivize different ways of using ODA for the least developed or more fragile coun- tries. Two key areas of change were 1) updating, clarifying, and streamlining existing ODA reporting, and 2) expanding ODA to bring in new activities and financial instruments (Develop- ment Initiatives 2017: 6). Accordingly, in 2016, OECD-DAC revised their rules for peace and security expenditures eligibility to 'better recognise the marginal, but actual developmental role that military actors sometimes play, notably in conflict situations, while clearly delineating it from their main peace and security function' (OECD 2020b: 3). These revisions sought to 'clarify ambiguities to ensure uniform, consistent statistical reporting, but also to approve the ODA- eligibility of development-related training for partner country military staff in limited topics' (OECD 2020b: 3).

The OECD-DAC has 'implemented the updated ODA rules on peace and security in the report- ing, issued a revised *ODA Casebook on Conflict, Peace and Security Activities*, and complemented the technical review of the ODA coefficient applied to UN peacekeeping operations' (OECD 2020b: 3). According to these new guidelines, the OECD-DAC expanded ODA's 'definition to include additional activities such as preventing violent extremism, migration management and military costs for the delivery of humanitarian relief' to 'potentially include more security-related activities … to encourage aid spending on SDG-16' (Möller-Loswick 2017). Moreover, OECD- DAC members may now report 15%, instead of the previous 7%, 'of what they contribute to UN peacekeeping in their ODA figures' (Möller-Loswick 2017).

There are concerns in the development circles over the risks of 'diverting aid more towards a military agenda for fighting wars rather than non-violent, preventative and developmental approaches' (Möller-Loswick 2017). Skepticism is targeted towards the fact that before the update of OECD-DAC's definition of ODA, there were 'limitations … on the direct funding of security- related activities … [presenting] difficulties for support to certain SSR activities (Fitz-Gerald 2012: 295). Fitz-Gerald (2012: 295) notes that donor countries like the UK, the Netherlands, and Canada, 'created new funding mechanisms which stood independent of ODA and could be used to support more comprehensive SSR' in order to 'circumvent some of the more restrictive

ODA criteria.' The critics warn that 'it is not immediately clear what further expanding the definition of aid to include more security-related costs would achieve,' as many activities that fall under SDG-16 would already count towards the ODA (Möller-Loswick 2017). They warn that the expansion of the definitions of ODA 'could lead to a squeeze on spending on activities such as peacebuilding or humanitarian relief – already inadequate – as donors seek to reach ODA targets while spending more on hard security' (Möller-Loswick 2017). The new definition of ODA containing certain security and defense costs, such as measures to prevent violent extremism and provide limited military training, may mean that 'the operational and tactical requirements of such measures are often outside the scope of many development agencies, encouraging partnerships with military or law enforcement agencies' (Bergenas & Mahoney 2016). Skeptics fear that this new definition will sidetrack donors from traditional development goals, such as education and gender equality (Bergenas & Mahoney 2016) and are concerned that 'donors' security interests are being prioritized at the expense of citizens in conflict-affected countries' (Möller-Loswick 2017). Nevertheless, it is important to draw attention to the fact that SSR aims to create professional security forces that work within the confines of democratic and rules-based frameworks. Therefore, investing in SSR does not necessarily mean creating larger security apparatus. For instance, smaller but well-trained staff can make a major difference, especially in post-conflict contexts, replacing the corrupt or dysfunctional security apparatus.

Another concern is that SDG-16, particularly Target 16.a, may be 'used by the EU to justify "train and equip" assistance to security forces to foster peace and development' (Möller-Loswick 2017; Tricot O'Farrell 2016). The argument is that such train and equip assistance may go into countries that are not necessarily interested in reforming their security institutions, such as Ethiopia and Sudan. This, in turn, would potentially lead to less peace and more insecurity by 'reinforcing the problems that have fuelled instability and displacement in the first place' (Möller-Loswick 2017; Tricot O'Farrell 2016).

A further concern about the SDG-16 is the difficulty of monitoring it due to 'the complexity and evolving nature of the issues to measure, their political sensitivity and the fact that traditionally National Statistical Offices (NSOs) have not focused on SDG-16 related issues' (SDG-16 Conference 2019: 3). For instance, due to 'the sensitive nature of SDG 16 … some countries cling to the notion of strongly upholding their sovereignty and government dominance without internal or external interference' (Hope 2020b: 67).

There are additional problems with the implementation of SDG-16 targets, such as 'inadequate capacity' of states, 'poor data and information' on security and justice sector indicators, 'inadequate delivery systems,' 'insufficient financing,' and 'lack of political will and leadership' (Hope 2020b: 67–70). For instance, measuring SDG-16 presents additional challenges due to it being a new goal that was not previously listed under the MDG framework (Milante et al. 2015). As noted by UNDP (2017: 6), '[G]overnance is a fairly new domain in official statistics, with few international standards defining its measurement and few countries and statistical offices having experience in producing governance statistics.' Therefore, coordination with a variety of stakeholders, including different governments, civil society organizations, academics, and experts to identify national and global indicators become important (UNDP 2017). This allows for the countries to 'ground the global agenda in their national realities and development priorities' (UNDP 2017: 37).

Subsequently, there is a need for harmonization of data collection methodologies across the world, along with the necessity of including 'youth, refugees and other vulnerable groups' in data collection (SDG-16 Conference 2019: 5). There are three specific challenges that NSOs need to overcome: independence 'to uphold the impartiality of statistics,' 'budgetary constraints,' and the use of 'robust, inclusive methodologies that meet international standards' (SDG-16 Conference 2019: 7). Especially on corruption, there is a 'need for a sound, clear and universal definition of corruption for analytical purposes, and for adopting methodologies that are sensitive to contexts' (SDG-16 Conference 2019: 8). As demonstrated by this section, despite its controversies, SDG-16 is 'key to achieving the transformative 2030 Agenda,' since it highlights 'seven tenets of strong institutions (effective, inclusive, responsive, participative, representative, accountable and transparent), as well as peaceful societies' (The Global Alliance 2019: 20).

CHAPTER 4

The Puzzle

As illustrated by the overview of the peace/security and development nexus and the content and controversies of SDG-16 sections above, the interconnectedness of security and development has been repeatedly acknowledged by the international community, especially since the end of the Cold War. Despite that, the international community had 'a deeply ambivalent attitude' towards dealing with complex intra-state conflicts, democratization processes, the economic viability of conflict-torn states, and the presence of organized crime networks (Wolff & Dursun-Özkanca 2012: 297). This ambivalence is substantiated by the incomplete track record of the international community on achieving peace, security, and development.

Three years after the adoption of the *2030 Agenda*, *Pathways for Peace*, a joint UN-WB study, highlighted both the role played by grievances in causing conflict and the importance of conflict prevention (UN & WB 2018). It called for prevention efforts to be sustained over time to 'address structural issues comprehensively, strengthen institutions, and adapt incentives for actions to manage conflict without violence' (UN & WB 2018: xxv). It also recommended prevention to be inclusive and to build broad partnerships across groups 'to identify and address grievances that fuel violence' and to 'target patterns of exclusion and institutional weaknesses that increase risk' (UN & WB 2018: xxv). According to the latest IEP report, 'the level of global peacefulness deteriorated' for the ninth time in the past 12 years, and violence has a cost of $14.5 trillion annually, which is equivalent to 10.6% of the world's economic activity (IEP 2020: 3). Furthermore, by 2030, over 60% of the world's poor will be living in countries affected by high levels of violence (OECD 2015; UN and WB 2018).

As discussed earlier, even though there are significant tendencies among technocrats for compartmentalizing the security and development realms, contemporary security problems and development challenges do not occur in isolation. They feed off of each other. Good governance of the security and justice sector is key to sustainable development (DCAF, OSCE/ODIHR & UN Women 2019). Integrated and multidimensional responses to development challenges, especially in contexts that are associated with conditions of fragility and violent conflict, tackling the challenging and long-term reforms early on, and reconceptualizing transitions to develop a more

---

How to cite this book chapter:
Dursun-Özkanca, O. 2021. *The Nexus Between Security Sector Governance/Reform and Sustainable Development Goal-16: An Examination of Conceptual Linkages and Policy Recommendations.* Pp. 27–29. London: Ubiquity Press. DOI: https://doi.org/10.5334/bcm.d. License: CC-BY-NC

nuanced understanding of the type of transition a country is undergoing emerge as central to SDGs and *Agenda 2030* (UNDP & Oxford Policy Management 2019: 6).

It is therefore of crucial importance that the international community simultaneously address issues of peace and security and development, as there are 'transnational challenges – terrorism, crime, and societal resiliency – that poison the well for economic development' (Bergenas & Mahoney 2016). Nevertheless, there is a gap in the literature linking development and security through a conceptual framework connecting SDG-16 with SSG/R, especially when it comes to oversight, accountability, and local ownership in SSR. SSG/R place emphasis on the concepts of oversight of armed forces and police forces, highlight accountability, transparency, and empowerment of people in the decision-making processes when it comes to reforming the armed forces and police units. In that sense, SSG/R is well-equipped to contribute to majority of the targets of SDG-16. Nevertheless, SSR-related targets are a subset of the targets under SDG-16. Consequently, the issues that are under the purview of SDG-16 require an in-depth analysis of the nexus between security and development, specifically connecting SDG-16 to SSG/R.

This topic is especially pertinent at this point in time, as the COVID-19 pandemic imposed additional problems for both peace/security and economic development and underscored the fundamental importance of human security. There are serious concerns with regards to reversed gains on economic development, social progress, and environmental sustainability made prior to the pandemic (#SDG16Plus 2020; Barbier & Burgess 2020). The pandemic devastated most economies around the world. The lockdown measures 'have ruptured the traditional arteries for foreign direct investment… with supply chains upended and trade volumes crashing' (The Economist Intelligence Unit 2020: 1). As stated by The Economist Intelligence Unit (2020: 1), 'Hospitality, tourism, retail, entertainment and transport (particularly airlines) have all suffered from sharp falls in demand,' and 'electricity consumption – a broad measure of economic activity' and oil demand has dropped drastically. It is estimated that the pandemic could cost the world more than US$10 trillion (Vos, Martin & Laborde 2020), and it had a particularly adverse effect on the developing countries in Africa and South Asia (Ahmed et al. 2020; Sumner, Ortiz-Juarez & Hoy 2020). To illustrate, it is expected that up to 400 million new poor are expected to live in extreme poverty, and over 500 million new poor expected to live under US$3.20 and US$5.50 (Sumner, Ortiz-Juarez & Hoy 2020). As reaffirmed in the latest High-Level Political Forum on Sustainable Development (HLPF) in July 2020, the pandemic 'is expected to push tens of millions of people back into extreme poverty and hunger' (ECOSOC 2020: 3).

Besides its harmful impact on economic development, the pandemic is also expected to have negative repercussions on peace and security. The pandemic is expected to have a negative impact on peace due to 'a new wave of tension and uncertainty' (IEP 2020: 2). The economic repercussions of the pandemic 'will likely have a severe impact on the way societies function,' leading to declining positive peace and increasing the risk of outbreaks of violence and conflict' (IEP 2020: 3). The pandemic is expected to increase the likelihood of conflicts around the world, as civil unrest in Europe is expected to rise 'as the looming recession bites' (IEP 2020: 3). Moreover, countries around the world may engage in a blame game, blaming others for the challenges they face (Leal Filho 2020), and 'famine conditions,' may create 'further stress on many fragile countries' in Africa (IEP 2020: 3). Furthermore, in response to COVID-19, several governments introduced laws that impinge on basic freedoms of their citizens. As the IEP (2020: 7) reports, 'The Safety and Security domain deteriorated on average, with 89 countries deteriorating and 70 improving.' There is a growing trend towards authoritarianism around the world, as reflected in deterioration in several indicators, such as 'political terror scale, police rate, and incarceration rate' (IEP 2020: 7). There are growing numbers of violent demonstrations and social unrest around the world, such as in Chile and Hong Kong, and 'the possibility of future violence remains high' (IEP 2020: 7).

Gender equality is key for the attainment of SDG-16 (DCAF, OSCE/ODIHR and UN Women 2019). Nevertheless, there are 'risks of regression in gender equality' (ECOSOC 2020: 3) due to the 'multi-faceted impact of the COVID-19 pandemic on women and girls, who … face increased levels of violence and exploitation' (ECOSOC 2020: 4). As stated by the HLPF 2020, there are deep concerns 'about the impact of high debt levels on countries' ability to withstand the impact of the COVID-19 shock and to invest in the implementation of the 2030 Agenda' (ECOSOC 2020: 7).

It is, therefore, safe to argue that the COVID-19 pandemic has convoluted and exacerbated the already-complex and multidimensional problems that the international community has been facing in accomplishing the SDGs. It created an unprecedented scale of threats to people's health, livelihood, dignity, which helped make it clear that health, economic, political, food, environmental, and community security are all deeply intertwined. This paper, therefore, seeks to fill the gap in the literature by incorporating the human security approach into the conceptual framework on the nexus between SSG/R and SDG-16. It holds that the latest developments bolster the value of the concept of human security in weaving closer connections between SSG/R and SDG-16.

CHAPTER 5

Conceptual Framework: SSG/R and SDG-16 Nexus

a. Commonalities between SSG/R and SDG-16

SDG-16 is intrinsically related to SSR, which seeks to ensure the safety of citizens to live their daily lives free from fear of attacks, criminal assault, or other forms of violence (UN 2018). In that sense, both focus on negative peace measures. SDG-16 also particularly seeks to change the culture as well as implement institutional reforms (SDG-16 Conference 2019: 9), which are central aspects to the SSR missions. As such, they both aim at establishing positive peace too. SDG-16 targets seek to improve institutions of the justice system, policymaking, and law enforcement. In that sense, SDG-16 and SSR share the same focus on the 'police, prosecutors, judges, prison system and ministries that deal with justice and policing' (TAP Network 2016: 15). SDG-16 highlights the need for having good SSG (Myrttinen 2019). They both focus on improving governance within national states. As illustrated by Table 2 below, promotion of the rule of law and equal access to justice (Target 16.3), the return of stolen assets, the reduction of arms flows, and fight against organized crime (Target 16.4), reduction of corruption (Target 16.5), accountability and transparency (Target 16.6), responsive, inclusive, participatory and representative decision making (Target 16.7), and strengthening of relevant national institutions for building capacity at all levels to prevent violence and combat terrorism and crime (Target 16.a) are among the many goals shared between SSG/R and SDG-16. There is an especially strong connection between Targets 16.3, 16.6, 16.7, 16.10, 16.a, and 16.b and SSG/R. Here, it is possible to identify a number of thematic issues that connect SSG/R with SDG-16, such as inclusivity, context specificity, and governance and institutionalization concepts of transparency, democratic oversight, accountability, legitimacy, and the rule of law.

How to cite this book chapter:
Dursun-Özkanca, O. 2021. *The Nexus Between Security Sector Governance/Reform and Sustainable Development Goal-16: An Examination of Conceptual Linkages and Policy Recommendations.* Pp. 31–37. London: Ubiquity Press. DOI: https://doi.org/10.5334/bcm.e. License: CC-BY-NC

Table 2: SSG/R and SDG-16 Commonalities.

	Inclusivity	Context Specificity	Transparency	Democratic Oversight	Accountability	Legitimacy	The Rule of Law
			SSG/R Thematic Concepts				
			Governance and Institutionalization				
Target 16.1	√	√	√		√		√
Target 16.2	√			√	√	√	√
Target 16.3	√		√	√	√	√	√
Target 16.4			√	√	√	√	√
Target 16.5			√	√	√	√	√
Target 16.6	√		√	√	√	√	√
Target 16.7	√	√	√	√	√	√	√
Target 16.8	√					√	√
Target 16.9	√		√			√	√
Target 16.10	√	√	√	√	√	√	√
Target 16.a	√	√	√	√	√	√	√
Target 16.b	√		√	√	√	√	√

i. Inclusivity

Inclusivity, which lies at the heart of SDG-16, is also key to the success of SSR and an important principle of SSG, as demonstrated by a relatively recent emphasis allocated to local ownership in the SSG/R literature. To have a successful outcome in both SSR and SSG, the participative approach is of the highest importance so that all the relevant stakeholders are involved in the reforms of the security sector and for accountability. Furthermore, illustrating the importance of inclusivity, *Agenda 2030* emphasizes that the SDGs aim to leave 'no one behind' (UNGA 2015: 3). Regarding inclusivity, '*who* is included (elites versus broader society); and around *what* (for instance, processes of decision-making versus outcomes),' emerge as important questions (Rocha Menocal 2015, italics in original). There is a sizable literature on the importance of inclusivity and the impact of exclusion and injustice on cultivating violent conflict (Collier & Hoeffler 2004; Cramer 2003; Donais & McCandless 2016; Evans 2012; Paffenholz 2014; Rocha Menocal 2015).

Inclusivity is encapsulated in numerous SDG-16 targets. Target 16.6 is directly related to effectiveness, accountability, and transparency, which are similarly emphasized in SSR, along with democratic oversight and assessment. To have public trust and legitimacy, it is of key importance that the different segments of the society feel included in the way public services, especially security infrastructure, are organized. Legitimacy is defined by OECD-DAC (2010: 7) as 'the extent that people regard [a political order, institution or actor] as satisfactory and believe that no available alternative would be vastly superior.' It is especially important for targets and indicators 16.2, 'End abuse, exploitations, trafficking and all forms of violence against and torture of children,' and 16.6.2, 'Percentage of the population satisfied with their last experience of public services' (UN Statistics Division 2016: 11). Every member of society needs to feel safe when it comes to trusting that the security sector will seek the best interest of all people in the society, such as children, as well as minorities and women. In that sense, Indicator 16.6.2 is closely related to Target 10.2 (social inclusion) (UN Statistics Division 2016: 23). These goals and targets support the concepts of accountability, legitimacy, local ownership, and democratic oversight that lie at the heart of SSG/R.

Moreover, Indicator 16.2.3 'Proportion of young women and men aged 18–29 years who experienced sexual violence by age 18' also emphasizes the inclusion of youth in protection against sexual violence. Inclusion is also highlighted by Target 16.7 'Ensure responsive, inclusive, participatory and representative decision-making at all levels' (UN Statistics Division 2016: 26). Representation and participation of all groups of the society in decision making is emphasized by this particular target. As noted by the UN Statistics Division (2016: 26), 'Fairer representation of all population groups in public service positions at all levels renders decision-making by public bodies more legitimate and more responsive to the concerns of the whole population.' Here, besides objective measures, perception-related subjective measures become similarly important in assessing the SDG-16.7. As noted by the UN Statistics Division (2016: 27), 'In cases where a group is very under-represented or has experienced historical discrimination, temporary special measures including minimum quotas on representation may be introduced to redress such discrimination.' This further supports the context-specific nature of Target 16.7.

Target 16.7 focuses on having inclusive, participatory, and representative decision making at all levels of public bodies. It is in line with the principles of good governance that are emphasized by the SSG. This target is of particular importance for a successful implementation of inclusivity in effective SSR, as it ensures a fairer representation of different population groups in these institutions and contributes to increased legitimacy and responsiveness to the concerns of all people in the population. For SSG/R purposes, special attention has to be paid to inclusion, participation, and representation of different groups of people in the judiciary, police, and military. Ensuring local ownership in SSR missions would positively contribute to the implementation of Target 16.7.

Inclusivity is once again pronounced by Target 16.9, 'By 2030, provide legal identity for all, including birth registration.' If people lack a legal identity, it is not procedurally feasible to envision their inclusion in any public debate or institution. Therefore, Target 16.9 is of key importance for the implementation of the principle of inclusivity. As noted by the UN Statistics Division (2016: 31), registration for legal identity is 'the first step in securing their recognition before the law, safeguarding … rights, and ensuring that any violation of these rights does not go unnoticed.' Secondly, it enables governments to 'effectively plan and budget for basic services' (TAP Network 2016: 11).

Another instance in which inclusivity is pronounced is through Target 16.a – 'Strengthen relevant national institutions, including through international cooperation, for building capacity at all levels, in particular in developing countries, to prevent violence and combat terrorism and crime' (UN Statistics Division 2016: 43). On 20 December 1993, the UN General Assembly Resolution 48/134 on 'National Institutions for the Promotion and Protection of Human Rights,' adopted an annex outlining 'the Principles relating to the Status of National Institutions,' also known as the *Paris Principles* (Council of Europe 2018). *The Paris Principles* called for the creation of independent national human rights institutions (NHRIs) by all UN member states. NHRIs are designed to be 'non-judicial, independent institutions created by states through their constitution or law, with the mandate to promote and protect human rights' (Council of Europe 2018).

The *Paris Principles* still leave a significant amount of leeway for the UN member states to decide the type of NHRI to best serve their domestic purposes. As noted by the Council of Europe (2018), 'In Europe, the most common models are ombudsman institutions, human rights commissions, hybrid institutions (which combine several mandates, including that of equality body), and human rights institutes and centres.' *The Paris Principles* set the benchmarks for the integrity, impartiality, and effectiveness of NHRIs in dealing with all human rights. An important component of *The Paris Principles* revolves around the concept of inclusion of national and international stakeholders, transparency, and accountability (the Council of Europe 2018). NHRIs 'operate and function independently from government' and 'address discrimination in all its forms, as well as to promote the protection of civil, political, economic, social and cultural rights' (UN Statistics Division 2016: 43). Effective NHRIs provide a link between government and civil society organizations and address the 'protection gap' between individual rights and government responsibilities (UN Statistics Division 2016: 43). NHRIs play a key role in 'monitoring, ensuring inclusion and participation, as well as in the domain of access to justice … bridg[ing] the link between sustainable development and human rights' (SDG-16 Conference 2019: 9).

Finally, Target 16.b too emphasizes inclusivity. This is clearly highlighted by its title 'Promote and enforce non-discriminatory laws and policies for sustainable development,' highlighting non-discrimination. This target emphasizes that non-discrimination and sustainable development go hand in hand with one another and is related to SDG Targets 10.2, 10.3, and 16.3.

ii. Context specificity

Besides inclusion, context specificity is another commonality between SSR and SDG-16. The features of the local environment are crucial for the success of both SSR and the attainment of the targets of SDG-16. Even though the universality principle is emphasized by both SSG and SDGs, it does not mean that specific context-related factors are going to be irrelevant to the implementation of SSG/R and SDG-16. In fact, in assessing the progress made on Target 16.1, 'Significantly reduce all forms of violence and related death rates everywhere,' there is a consensus on the need to classify the deaths from violence between intentional homicide and conflict-related deaths. Especially for conflict-related deaths, not all countries around the world experience conflict. Therefore, context specificity becomes important for determining 'the scope of these threats,' and effectively mitigating the dangers caused by them (UN Statistics Division 2016: 9).

Context specificity is once again highlighted by Target 16.7, 'Ensure responsive, inclusive, participatory and representative decision-making at all levels.' To illustrate, each country has a different track record of different groups of people that are under-represented in decision making. By using context specificity, the international community can more effectively and efficiently determine the target groups, such as people with disabilities, members of different ethnic groups, LGBTQ communities, religious groups, and linguistic groups.

Target 16.10 also emphasizes context specificity in the context of ensuring public access to information for the protection of fundamental freedoms. It acknowledges the role played by national legislation. Therefore, in order to take the necessary measures against deficiencies, it is important to determine each country's track record on access to information, fundamental rights implementation, and human rights violations committed especially against journalists, human rights defenders, and trade unionists (UN Statistics Division 2016).

iii. Governance and institutionalization

Aside from inclusivity and context specificity, governance and institutionalization have been similarly emphasized by SSG/R and SDG-16. Creation and strengthening of institutions are important elements for governing better. As illustrated below, they can be achieved through transparency, democratic oversight, accountability, legitimacy, and the rule of law.

1. Transparency, democratic oversight, accountability, and legitimacy

One important principle of good governance is transparency, which is similarly emphasized by both SSG/R and SDG-16. For instance, Targets 16.6 and 16.10 are directly related to the concept of transparency. Target 16.6 is titled, 'Develop effective, accountable and transparent institutions at all levels.' Target 16.10, 'Ensure public access to information and protect fundamental freedoms, in accordance with national legislation and international agreements,' is directly related to the principle of transparency. These two targets are related to public trust in institutions, an important aspect of successful SSR implementation. Transparency is one of the main principles of SSG (DCAF 2015). It is defined as information being 'freely available and accessible to those who will be affected by decisions and their implementation' (DCAF 2015: 3).

Democratic oversight is a 'precondition for accountability' (Gill 2020: 4). Accountability, another important principle of SSG, is vital for healing the 'wounds of past abuses' and in establishing enduring peace (SDG-16 Conference 2019: 7). It 'means that people will be held responsible for their actions and for how they perform their duties' (The Centre for Integrity in the Defence Sector (CIDS) 2014: 8). It is typically guaranteed by the effective implementation of the rule of law. As explained in greater detail in the final section of this manuscript, oversight and accountability have important implications for the legitimacy of the security sector in the eyes of the people and are equally emphasized by SDG-16. Transparency, oversight, and accountability enhance perceptions of public security and add to legitimacy of the police (Hryniewicz 2011). As indicated in Table 2, Targets 16.3, 16.4, 16.5, 16.6, 16.7, 16.10, 16.a, and 16.b are directly related to transparency, democratic oversight, accountability, and legitimacy.

2. The rule of law

Final commonalities between SSG/R and SDG-16 include the goals of enforcing the rule of law and further institutionalization. For instance, reduction of violence (Target 16.1), ending abuse, exploitation, trafficking and all forms of violence and torture against children (Target 16.2), promotion of the rule of law at the national and international levels, and equal access to justice for all (Target 16.3), as well as reduction of small arms and combatting against organized crime (Target 16.4) and corruption (Target 16.5) are all shared between SSG/R and SDG-16, and revolve around the concept of the rule of law. It is well-established that 'access to justice empowers the poor and marginalized to claim their rights' (SDG-16 Conference 2019: 6). Therefore, the 'provision of free legal aid services to all' emerges as an important agenda item, as do alternative dispute resolution mechanisms (SDG-16 Conference 2019: 15). Ensuring institutional integrity, transparency, anti-corruption mechanisms, facilitation of investigations of criminal activities, corruption, and money laundering is important for SSG/R as well as for SDG-16. Similarly, as noted by OECD-DAC (2007: 5), 'control over the production, export, import and transit of small arms and light weapons, [and] the development of institutional structures for policy guidance, research and monitoring' are within the purview of SSR due to their implications on the rule of law.

Institutionalization, which is emphasized in Target 16.a, 'Strengthen relevant national institutions, including through international cooperation, for building capacity at all levels, in particular in developing countries, to prevent violence and combat terrorism and crime,' is directly related to the SSG/R's core mission. It is similarly emphasized by both Target 16.6, which seeks to 'develop effective, accountable and transparent institutions,' and Target 16.8 on global institutions. Finally, the effectiveness of inter-institutional cooperation and coordination is expected to determine the success of the outcomes in both SSR and SDG-16. Multi-stakeholder and 'whole-of-government' approaches are key to both SSG/R and SDG-16 (OECD-DAC 2007: 11).

b. Differences between SSG/R and SDG-16

While there are many commonalities between SSG/R and SDG-16, there are also a few differences between the two, especially in terms of the emphasis given to certain concepts. One of the major differences between SSR and SDG-16 is that the SDGs, including SDG-16, are universal in focus, whereas SSR has been primarily focusing on developing and post-conflict countries, typically ignoring the developed parts of the world. SSG, on the other hand, seeks to reaffirm the principles of good governance in the management of the security sector universally.

Secondly, the focus on combatting organized crime and reducing illicit financial and arms flows is more prevalent in SDG-16 than it is in SSG/R. While SSG/R focus on transparency and the rule of law, they do not directly tackle the issues of organized crime and illicit financial and arms flows, except for the cases of DDR conducted in post-conflict contexts, which seeks to rehabilitate former combatants and involve initiatives pertaining to small arms and light weapons (SALW) (Wulf 2011: 340). Therefore, Target 16.4, 'By 2030 significantly reduce illicit financial and arms flows, strengthen recovery and return of stolen assets, and combat all forms of organized crime,' does not fully fall under the direct purview of SSG/R. Having said that, if conducted properly and applied in a local context in the West and Global South, SSG/R would ensure that organized crime and illicit financial and arms flow problems are under control. Otherwise, SALW initiatives and DDR provide somewhat of an ancillary link between SSR and Target 16.4.

Thirdly, Target 16.8 is another difference between SDG-16 and SSR. Even though Target 16.8 places a special role on inclusivity, it does so at the global level. Target 16.8 is defined as 'Broaden and strengthen the participation of developing countries in the institutions of global governance' (UN Statistics Division 2016: 29). In other words, whereas Target 16.7 focuses at the local level in each member state of the UN, Target 16.8 assesses whether different countries are represented in international organizations with a global mandate, such as the IMF, the World Bank, the Prepara-tory Commission for the Comprehensive Nuclear-Test-Ban Treaty Organization (CTBTO), Inter-national Atomic Energy Agency (IAEA), Organisation for the Prohibition of Chemical Weapons (OPCW), and the World Trade Organization (WTO) (UN Statistics Division 2016). It emphasizes the importance of participation of all countries in the global financial-economic structures and the rules-based system. SSR, on the other hand, can be more developed-country initiated and may be more in line with the security interests of Western governments, whereas SDG-16 seeks to empower the developing countries more. This does not mean to suggest that SSG/R are against participation of developing countries in the global governance structures, but it simply indicates that this issue does not receive priority in SSG/R planning.

Fourthly, Target 16.9, 'By 2030 provide legal identity for all including free birth registrations,' is not under the purview of SSR. While provision of legal identity for all would be a preliminary requirement for a successful justice reform and contribute to the overall rule of law in a country, it is not directly related to the SSR mission. Having said that, it is important to acknowledge that provision of legal identity would be essential in making sure that people's rights and freedoms are protected by the actors of the security sector. For instance, 'Many children have no legal identity, which is a risk factor for trafficking or exclusion from public services' (SDG-16 Conference 2019: 7). Since it is a precondition for ensuring an equal implementation of the rule of law, it is still some-what related to SSG/R.

Moreover, Target 16.10, 'Ensure public access to information and protect fundamental free-doms, in accordance with national legislation and international agreements,' is in line with the concepts of accountability and transparency, which are important principles of good governance cherished by SSG/R. However, it is possible to make the argument that the way this target is framed in SDG-16 is more closely in line with the concept of human security than with SSG/R, because it limits itself to the access of information with regards to the security and justice sectors and has a broader focus on fundamental freedoms. As reported in previous empirical studies, when it comes to implementation, SSR missions in Bosnia-Herzegovina, Kosovo, Georgia, and the Palestinian Territories prioritized the state rather than the people (Bouris 2012; Dursun-Özkanca & Vandemoortele 2014; Kunz & Valasek 2012; Simons 2012). Target 16.10's emphasis is there-fore more directly aligned with human security's emphasis on transparency, empowerment of the people, and accountability.

Nonetheless, Target 16.10 still aligns well with the main principles of SSG/R, due to its emphasis on the concepts of accountability and transparency. In fact, during the first phase of a post-conflict SSR process, enacting laws that ensure guaranteed access to information is a priority. During the more advanced phases of the SSR, developing the civilian capacity further through parliamentary oversight, civil society, freedom of the media, and creation of epistemic communities to exercise formal and informal oversight powers become priorities. Without a successful first phase of SSR, countries may not achieve successful implementation of further SSG/R. For instance, research on Indonesian and Nigerian parliaments as political actors and arenas of military reform revealed that important political battles of the reform process have been waged for passing laws that ensure guaranteed access to information. However, when this was not successful, further progress for SSR was hampered (Rüland et al. 2012). Given that the state is the only entity that can guarantee the implementation of human rights principles, such as freedom of access to information, SSG/R, if successfully implemented, can substantially contribute to the attainment of Target 16.10, especially with regards to access to security-related information.

Target 16.b, 'Promote and enforce non-discriminatory laws and policies for sustainable development,' is not directly related to the SSR mission, even though the rule of law and non-discrimination are important foundational principles in SSG. While non-discriminatory laws and policies are prioritized, there is no direct reference to sustainable development in typical SSR missions. As explained in the subsequent section, this target aligns especially well with the concept of human security's freedom from fear, as it would eliminate discrimination in the legal system based on race, sex, gender, religion, and ethnicity, and freedom from want, and it would promote sustainable development.

Furthermore, even though some emphasize SSR's people-centered nature (Schnabel & Farr 2012), comparatively speaking, putting people first is more emphasized in SDG-16 than in SSG/R, where the focus is primarily on the institutions of the state. Having said that, as noted in the previous section, institutionalization plays an important role in both SSG/R and SDG-16. This is evident in the SDG-16's main emphasis on building 'effective, accountable and inclusive institutions at all levels.' SSR practice tends to focus more on national security rather than human security. It is mainly top-down rather than bottom-up. The main goal in SSR is institution building. Institutions, by nature and design, are maintained by the states. As criticized by many scholars of SSR, SSR is 'state-centric' both with regards to its definition of security and the providers of security (Bouris 2012; Dursun-Özkanca & Vandemoortele 2014; Kunz & Valasek 2012; Simons 2012). SSR activities should not aim 'to secure the state at the expense of the people' and instead should emphasize the need to protect human security (Dursun-Özkanca & Vandemoortele 2014: 149). 'Due to state-centrism, most SSR funding from international donors has gone to "reforming" formal state security institutions, such as the police and armed forces,' while ignoring oversight bodies and non-state security and justice providers (Kunz & Valasek 2012: 125).

Finally, whereas SDG-16 emphasizes longer-term goals, SSR programming may suffer from short-sighted thinking due to donor interests. Another fundamental difference between SDG-16 and SSG/R is the emphasis placed on public perceptions of safety. While perceptions of security play a significant role in SDG-16, they do not play much of a role in SSR. As illustrated by the next section, with regards to many of these differences between SDG-16 and SSG/R, human security is fittingly situated to better align SSG/R with SDG-16 and its targets. While SSG/R and SDG-16 share and emphasis on peace, security, institution-building as well as justice and human rights, SSR does not directly share the front-and-center emphasis placed by human security and SDG-16 on sustainable development.

CHAPTER 6

How to Better Tie SSG/R and SDG-16 Together

This section introduces the concept of human security as a way to better tie SSG/R and SDG-16 and discusses how the concept has evolved over time. Human security places a key emphasis on the security-development nexus (Steiner 2019), arguably more so than SSR. It holds that 'sustainable development and sustaining peace are two sides of the same coin' (Steiner 2019). It maintains, 'the safety and economic well-being (freedom from fear and freedom from want) are key ingredients of a stable society with a promising future' (Schnabel 2012: 31). In that sense, as demonstrated below, human security provides a helpful bridge between SDG-16 and SSG/R.

a. Human security: An introduction

The concept of human security has emerged from the UNDP's 1994 Human Development Report, titled *New Dimensions of Human Security*, and has evolved over time. Human development seeks to enhance the lives of humans, which makes the emphasis on human security central (The Commission on Human Security 2003). Human security is typically defined as freedom from fear and freedom from want, as it emphasizes 'first, safety from such chronic threats as hunger, disease and repression,' and 'second, … protection from sudden and hurtful disruptions in the patterns of daily life – whether in homes, in jobs or in communities' (UNDP 1994: 23).

The concept of human security not only emphasizes the security of the individual, but also highlights the importance of development. It 'puts people at the centre of development,' 'regards economic growth as a means not an end,' and places an emphasis on sustainable development by protecting 'the life opportunities of future generations as well as the present generations' (UNDP 1994: 4). Referring to the notion of 'peace dividends,' UNDP (1994: 58) suggests that human security contains seven components: economic, food, health, environment, personal, community, and political security. Thus, it proposes a more comprehensive assessment of the well-being of the people by expanding the focus on security to include threats to human needs and well-being, such as diseases, environmental threats, economic threats. It includes the assumption that

How to cite this book chapter:
Dursun-Özkanca, O. 2021. *The Nexus Between Security Sector Governance/Reform and Sustainable Development Goal-16: An Examination of Conceptual Linkages and Policy Recommendations.* Pp. 39–46. London: Ubiquity Press. DOI: https://doi.org/10.5334/bcm.f. License: CC-BY-NC

such threats 'can trigger direct and structural violence, possibly leading to armed violence' caus-ing a vicious cycle (Baldassini et al. 2018: 16). Therefore, the argument it holds is that if individu-als and communities are free from fear and want, 'conflict can be mitigated' (Baldassini et al. 2018: 16). In that sense, human security represents a shift from a state-centric security approach (UNDP 1994).

The 1995 Copenhagen declaration, published following the World Summit, officially embraced human security as a guiding concept for development work (Bueger & Vennesson 2009). Fol-lowing a brief pause in attention to the concept, Canada introduced the concept in the UNSC at the end of the 1990s (Baldassini et al. 2018). In 1999, the Human Security Network (HSN) was established under the leadership of Austria, Norway, and Canada as a result of the anti-landmine movement; it seeks to promote 'the concept of human security as a feature of national and inter-national policies, and in particular within the United Nations and in cooperation with academia and civil society' (PreventionWeb 2020). Its members include Austria, Chile, Costa Rica, Greece, Ireland, Jordan, Mali, Norway, Panama, Slovenia, Switzerland, and Thailand, with South Africa participating as an observer (PreventionWeb 2020).

Since then, human security has steadily acquired attention from the international community. It is one of the prime examples of 'epistemic learning,' or the emergence of a consensus among policymakers on a novel way to respond to security challenges (Faleg 2012: 161). The Commis-sion on Human Security was launched at the 2000 UN Millennium Summit. In 2001, the OECD acknowledged the central role of human security in security-development nexus (Baldassini et al. 2018). The Commission aims to empower and protect people, and 'focus on what can be done in the short and the long run to enhance the opportunities for eliminating insecurities across the world' (The Commission on Human Security 2003: iv). In September 2002, under the initia-tive of Japan, the Commission on Human Security created more momentum behind the concept internationally (Inter-American Institute of Human Rights 2020). A year later, the Commission on Human Security published its widely cited *Human Security Now* report (The Commission on Human Security 2003).

The *Human Security Now* report emphasizes that 'the broad range of interconnected issues,' such as conflict and poverty, require human security's involvement to protect 'people during vio-lent conflict and in post-conflict situations,' to defend 'people who are forced to move,' to over-come 'economic insecurities,' to guarantee 'the availability of essential healthcare,' and to ensure 'the elimination of illiteracy and educational deprivation' (The Commission on Human Security 2003: iv). Regarding human security's emphasis on protection and empowerment, the Commis-sion on Human Security (2003: 10) notes that 'protection strategies' are set up by various state and non-state actors to 'shield people from menaces,' whereas 'empowerment strategies enable people to develop resilience to difficult conditions.' Human security creates 'political, social, environ-mental, economic, military and cultural systems that together give people the building blocks of survival, livelihood and dignity' (The Commission on Human Security 2003: 4). The latest panel held by the UNTFHS in June 2020 confirms this by noting that the goal of human security is to 'break through silos that constrain or prevent the type of integrated thinking necessary to address the scope and scale of today's human insecurities' (UNTFHS 2020).

Human security was referenced as a core principle for UN activities in *the Report of the UN High-Level Panel on Threats, Challenges and Change* (UNGA 2004), following the attempts by the 2000 and 2005 Reports of then UN Secretary-General Kofi Annan *We the People* and *In Larger Freedom* 'to institutionalize human security' (Bueger & Vennesson 2009: 18). *The Report of the UN High-Level Panel on Threats, Challenges and Change* (UNGA 2004: 15), for instance, acknowledges that the UN founders were predominantly preoccupied with state security when they created the organization, but adds that 'they also understood well … the indivisibility of security, economic development and human freedom.'

The UN General Assembly Resolution 66/290 (UNGA 2012: 1) defines human security as 'an approach to assist Member States in identifying and addressing widespread and cross-cutting challenges to the survival, livelihood and dignity of their people' and outlines the following components of human security that are indicated in Table 3.

Table 3: Human Security Components.

(a) The right of people to live in freedom and dignity, free from poverty and despair. All individuals, in particular vulnerable people, are entitled to freedom from fear and freedom from want, with an equal opportunity to enjoy all their rights and fully develop their human potential;
(b) Human security calls for people-centred, comprehensive, context-specific and prevention-oriented responses that strengthen the protection and empowerment of all people and all communities;
(c) Human security recognizes the interlinkages between peace, development and human rights, and equally considers civil, political, economic, social and cultural rights;
(d) The notion of human security is distinct from the responsibility to protect and its implementation;
(e) Human security does not entail the threat or the use of force or coercive measures. Human security does not replace State security;
(f) Human security is based on national ownership. Since the political, economic, social and cultural conditions for human security vary significantly across and within countries, and at different points in time, human security strengthens national solutions which are compatible with local realities;
(g) Governments retain the primary role and responsibility for ensuring the survival, livelihood and dignity of their citizens. The role of the international community is to complement and provide the necessary support to Governments, upon their request, so as to strengthen their capacity to respond to current and emerging threats. Human security requires greater collaboration and partnership among Governments, international and regional organizations and civil society;
(h) Human security must be implemented with full respect for the purposes and principles enshrined in the Charter of the United Nations, including full respect for the sovereignty of States, territorial integrity and non-interference in matters that are essentially within the domestic jurisdiction of States. Human security does not entail additional legal obligations on the part of States.

Source: UNGA (2012: 1–2).

All in all, human security emphasizes both protection and empowerment, pays special attention to the most vulnerable, and recognizes that problems rarely occur in isolation and that they are almost always interdependent (Stern & Öjendal 2010). It acknowledges that there are no one-size-fits-all solutions to problems around the world. As the next section illustrates, due to its scope, human security has a great potential to serve as a linkage between SSR/SSG and SDG-16.

b. Human security as a linkage between SSG/R and SDG-16

Reduction of violence is a shared goal between SSR, human security, and SDG-16. Promotion of the rule of law, access to justice, institutional reform, and combatting corruption goals are similarly shared between the three. Human security focuses on the 'insecurities that threaten human survival or the safety of daily life, or imperil the natural dignity of men and women, or expose human beings to the uncertainty of disease and pestilence, or subject vulnerable people to abrupt penury related to economic downturns' (The Commission on Human Security 2003: 8). As noted by the Commission on Human Security (2003: 8), human security 'supplements the expansionist perspective of human development by directly paying attention to what are sometimes called "downside risks."' Reflecting on the relationship between human security and human development, the Commission on Human Security (2003: 8) notes that while there are no contradictions between human security and human development, 'the emphasis and priorities are quite different in the cautious perspective of human security from those typically found in the relatively sanguine and upward-oriented literature of the human focus of development approaches.' The Commission maintains that the focus on human security calls for attention to be paid to 'downturns with security' and 'the adversity of persistent insecurity of those whom the growth process leaves behind, such as the displaced worker or the perennially unemployed' (The Commission on Human Security 2003: 8).

A careful examination of *The Agenda 2030* reveals that it closely incorporates important elements of the human security concept. For instance, it emphasizes that the SDGs have a universal focus, and they aim to leave 'no one behind' (UNGA 2015: 3). Human security's people-centered approach, summarized in its mantra of 'leave no one behind,' is a good starting point for bridging between SDG-16 and SSG/R. It is 'an essential tool to realize the core ambition of the 2030 Agenda' (Steiner 2019). 'Leave no one behind' is also becoming the mantra of the SDGs. *Agenda 2030* declares, 'As we embark on this great collective journey, we pledge that no one will be left behind' (UNGA 2015: 3). It also adds, 'Recognizing that the dignity of the human person is fundamental, we wish to see the Goals and targets met for all nations and peoples and for all segments of society' (UNGA 2015: 3).

Through its emphasis on empowerment, two targets that human security would effectively support are Target 16.8, 'Broaden and strengthen the participation of developing countries in the institutions of global governance,' and Target 16.10, 'Ensure public access to information and protect fundamental freedoms, in accordance with national legislation and international agreements.' The UN and WB (2018: xxvii) emphasize the importance of 'a people-centered approach,' 'mainstreaming citizen engagement in development programs and local conflict resolution to empower underrepresented groups such as women and youth' in achieving SDG-16. While both SDG-16 and human security hold the 'people-centered' approach and 'leave no one behind' principle dear to their heart, the SSG/R literature does not pay direct attention to these elements.

Furthermore, the SDGs have a complex implementation process, involving 'national ownership, flexibility, innovation, political acumen, high quality technical support and a collective, multi-stakeholder effort at all levels' (The Global Alliance 2019: 20). While these principles are similarly shared by SSR and SSG on paper, through its multi-stakeholder and multidimensional approach and emphasis on 'leaving no one behind,' human security would offer value-added solutions when it comes to ensuring that SSG/R more effectively contributes to SDG-16 targets.

A key factor that determines whether SSR and SDG-16 will be successful or not is effective inter-institutional cooperation and coordination. As suggested by the UN and WB (2018: xxvi), 'A coherent strategy that can be sustained over time demands levels of integrated planning and implementation that are often challenging to development, security, humanitarian, and political actors.' Hence, having a 'sustained, inclusive, and targeted prevention' coordinated effectively by these actors is critical (UN & WB 2018: xxvi). Human security's emphasis on inclusivity, prevention, and multi-stakeholder and comprehensive approach would aptly serve the goal of implementing SDG-16 targets. This is especially true for Target 16.a, as it focuses on strengthening national institutions through international cooperation for capacity building on prevention of violence and counterterrorism.

Nevertheless, some scholars are concerned that 'greater policy coherence and harmonisation among donors may lead to the subordination of development concerns to those of security and that ODA may thus be instrumentalised by donors to serve their geostrategic interests' (Tschirgi 2005, quoted in Thede 2013: 793). Tschirgi (2005: 12), for instance, notes that 'policy coherence is still at a high level of abstraction' and adds that conflict sensitivity has not been mainstreamed into development assistance. Another group of critical scholars attracts attention to the contradictions between 'the aid effectiveness agenda and the new emphasis on security in development' (Brown

2011, quoted in Thede 2013: 794; Fukuda-Parr 2010). Thede (2013: 796) argues that 'increasing convergence of the content, mechanisms, criteria and delivery of official aid among donors under the umbrella concept of "coherence"' leads to the subordination of development to diplomatic, military and trade concerns; and narrows 'the potential space for Southern governments to opt for a different set of development objectives.' Some argue that major international organizations, such as the WB, hold a 'security first' perspective for post-conflict peacebuilding processes (Krause & Jütersonke 2005; Schwarz 2005). Human security's comprehensive multidimensional approach would help to effectively respond to such criticisms, as it emphasizes both development and security at the same time.

The focus on local ownership is also highly essential for the success of the SSR in contributing to SDG-16 (Burt 2016). The incorporation of national- and local-level actors and policies in SSR is 'the key to sustainability' of SSR programming (Burt 2016: 7). Otherwise, international actors run the risk of failing to make progress in SSR unsustainable 'once project funds expire' or when 'national authorities that feel no ownership over the process' abandon it (Burt 2016: 7). Therefore, human security's inclusive, comprehensive, and multi-stakeholder approach would benefit SSG/R as well as SDG-16, helping address the gaps in SSR implementation and facilitating the accomplishment of SDG-16 targets more efficiently.

The 2008 Report of the UN Secretary-General was consequential in linking the concept of SSR with human security (UNSG 2008). Like SSR, the human security concept 'is a product of the progressive understanding and new security thinking that emerged from the end of the Cold War' (Schnabel & Farr 2012: 4). The 2008 Report of the UN Secretary-General notes, 'There are no quick fixes for establishing effective and accountable security institutions' and that it is a 'long-term process' to 'build a world in which men and women can live their lives and raise their children in dignity, free from hunger and the fear of violence, oppression of injustice' (UNSG 2008: 19). It is important to acknowledge that human security cannot be achieved in the absence of well-functioning state structures, which is an aspect that is addressed by successful SSG/R.

SSR's main raison d'être is to ensure that 'a nation's security institutions are effective, provide for the safety and security of the population and the state, and are overseen and controlled by civil society organisations and democratically elected representatives' (Schnabel 2012: 31). As such, SSG/R seek to 'ensure that the security sector offers protection from external and internal threats without itself becoming a threat, resulting in an environment that is safer and less prone to violence and instability and thus encourages economic growth, poverty reduction and human development' (Schnabel 2012: 31). Therefore, SSR's benefits can theoretically be experienced by both security and development circles, as 'safety and economic well-being are key ingredients of a stable society with a promising future,' and that SSR aims to have a 'security sector [that] offers protection from external and internal threats without itself becoming a threat' (Baldassini et al. 2018: 12).

While this is the way it is supposed to be on paper, SSR has lost touch with its development origins (Farr, Schnabel & Krupanski 2012). SSR was a 'late-coming player to the old and arguably overcrowded development field' (Farr, Schnabel & Krupanski 2012: 328). The coordination between SSR and development implementers has been weak, leading to gaps in SSR implementation in terms of the insights derived from development goals and government development plans (Farr, Schnabel & Krupanski 2012: 327). The development community similarly fails to integrate SSR approaches in planning and design of their missions (Farr, Schnabel & Krupanski 2012). Therefore, 'in reality, and particularly in post-conflict societies, SSR's security mandate has been more pronounced than its development mandate' (Baldassini et al. 2018; Schnabel 2012: 31). As Schnabel (2012: 65) notes, SSR predominantly focuses on 'security dividends, while development dividends remain unspecified or vaguely defined as implicit and immeasurable outcomes of improved security conditions.'

To address these deficiencies, 'early community-based and consultative assessments of populations' development and security needs should be conducted jointly, so that the results can inform both development and security interventions' (Farr, Schnabel & Krupanski 2012: 327). Human security is positioned well to fulfil that recommendation. Human security recognizes that challenges are complex and interlinked, requiring an integrated, multidimensional, multi-stakeholder approach to development and complex problems. It holds that vulnerabilities must be tackled together by both development and security actors. While the SDGs have the same recognition (Steiner 2019), SSG/R do not emphasize the multidimensional and integrated approach as much, giving human security a comparative advantage for serving as a link between the SDG-16 and SSG/R.

Human security protects and empowers people. The same is true for SSR and SDG-16. But, comparatively speaking, SSR focuses on a specific niche of specialized SSG and is more unidimensional or security heavy than SDG-16 and human security. This does not mean to imply that SSR's aims and modalities conflict with the human security paradigm. It simply means that the multidimensional aspect of phenomena and the development side is more pronounced in the case of SDG-16 and human security. Incorporating human security would, therefore, ensure that there is an added emphasis on achieving development and security simultaneously, and help to glue SSG/R and SDG-16 in a more seamless manner.

Directly referring to freedoms from want and fear, which are heavily emphasized by the human security approach, *Agenda 2030* declares:

> In these Goals and targets, we are setting out a supremely ambitious and transformational vision. We envisage a world free of poverty, hunger, disease and want, where all life can thrive. We envisage a world free of fear and violence. A world with universal literacy. A world with equitable and universal access to quality education at all levels, to health care and social protection, where physical, mental and social well-being are assured (UNGA 2015: 3).

Targets 16.1 and 16.2 are directly related to the concept of human security, especially freedom from fear, as they call for the reduction of all forms of violence everywhere and ending abuse, exploitation, trafficking and all forms of violence against and torture of children, respectively. As noted by the UN Statistics Division (2016: 2), 'Security from violence is a pre-requisite for individuals to enjoy a safe and active life and for societies and economies to develop freely.' Moreover, SSG/R place high importance on Target 16.3, promotion of the rule of law and equal access to justice for all, and so does human security. Target 16.9, provision of legal identity for all, is important for a systematic application of the rule of law and for human security's emphasis on protection and empowerment.

Referring to the importance of both state-centric understanding of security and a people-centered understanding of it, the Report of the UN Secretary-General (UNSG 2013: 4) notes:

> The objective of security sector reform is to help ensure that people are safer through the enhanced effectiveness and accountability of security institutions operating under civilian control within a framework of the rule of law and human rights. Provision of security is a core function of the State. In many contexts, security institutions, such as the military and the police, are the most visible representatives of the State for the general public. Thus effective, accountable and professional security institutions can have a defining and positive impact on people's confidence in the State. In some contexts, however, security institutions are incapable of protecting populations against threats. In others, security providers not only fail to protect individuals and communities, they may marginalize, exclude or even prey on the very populations they are entrusted to protect.

Target 16.4 aims at reducing illicit financial and arms flows, strengthening the recovery and return of stolen assets and combating all forms of organized crime. On this topic, the Report of the

UN Secretary-General in 2013 emphasizes the need to incorporate a human security approach in SSR by stating (UNSG 2013: 5):

> [T]he security of the State and the state of security (of individuals and communities) are mutually interdependent; in other words, we have learned that when populations are not secure, neither is the State. This poses an important challenge to the typical State-centric, post-conflict approach to security sector reform and calls for approaches that combine the central role of the State with its ultimate dependence on, and linkages to, the security and safety of individuals and communities. Current approaches to security sector reform have been confronted with a proliferation of transnational threats, including trafficking in humans, drugs and arms; terrorism; insurgency; climate change and environmental degradation; organized crime and armed violence; and cybercrime. This has led to the realization that no single State can, on its own, meet these transborder challenges, and points to the need for increased cooperation across borders.

As the UN Secretary-General's report (UNSG 2013) emphasizes, transnational problems require international cooperation. Therefore, human security, through its heavy emphasis on epistemic communities internationally, can help address transnational threats such as organized crime networks and illicit financial and arms trafficking in a more effective way. For instance, the UN and other international organizations, non-governmental organizations, as well as the groupings of states under the leadership of Japan and Canada help share norms and values that are associated with human security. The latest UNSC Resolution adopted on SSR too 'reiterates the importance of sharing experiences, best practices and lessons learned, knowledge and expertise on security sector reform among Members States, and regional and subregional organizations, expert institutions including academia and research organizations, and relevant stakeholders including women and youth organisations,' and also 'encourages a deepening of South-South exchange and cooperation' (UNSC 2020b: 8).

With regard to Target 16.5, which seeks to reduce corruption, human security's goals of improving the quality of life of individuals and empowerment would place an important emphasis on this target. Corruption has a 'direct negative impact on the social fabric, including in the provision of health and education, as well as in the protection of other basic human rights' (Tavanti & Stachowicz-Stanusch 2013: 2). Similarly, anti-corruption is an important part of good governance that is emphasized by SSG/R. Previous studies have established the inverse correlation between corruption and human security (Durojave 2010; Hassan 2020; Tavanti & Stachowicz-Stanusch 2013). Human security's collaborative, multidimensional, and multi-sectoral approach would effectively help address multiple dimensions of corruption, contributing to both Targets 16.5 and 16.b as well as SSR. Target 16.b focuses on promotion and enforcement of non-discriminatory laws and policies for sustainable development. Fight against corruption becomes important for achieving this target too, so does provision of legal identity, establishment of rule of law, and empowerment of individuals that are emphasized by human security.

One of the key components of SDG-16 is the emphasis put on the role of perceptions, especially of security and insecurity. This seems to make the concept of human security more central for the implementation stage of the SDGs. Whereas SDG-16 takes into consideration people's perception of security/insecurity, SSG/R normally look at assessment using more objective criteria. Public perceptions of safety do not play much of a direct role in SSG/R. In that sense, there are more commonalities between SDG-16 and human security with regards to the subjective interpretations of security. Human security can, therefore, serve as an important tool in fully connecting SSG/R with SDG-16, by emphasizing not only the objective but also the subjective nature of security. The emphasis on objective as well as subjective security assessment would have positive repercussions for transparency, accountability, and legitimacy, concepts that are central to the success of SSG/R (Dursun-Özkanca 2014). Illustrating this linkage, the Global Alliance (2019: 62) notes, institutions of 'local and regional governments [which] have the responsibility for delivering basic services and public goods … can gain increased importance in situations of insecurity, conflict or lack of trust in national governments (or where there is no functioning central government).' Therefore, attributing increased emphasis on perceptions would contribute to the overall rule of law, peace, and justice that SDG-16 aims to accomplish. For instance, it would contribute to Targets 16.6 and 16.7, which seek to develop effective, accountable, and transparent institutions at all levels, and ensure responsive, inclusive, participatory, and representative decision-making at all levels, respectively.

Finally, long-term goals are arguably more pronounced in human security, SDG-16, and SSG, whereas SSR efforts have the tendency to focus on short-term goals. In that sense too, human security is better positioned to connect SDG-16 with SSG/R and help SSR acquire a longer-term perspective in service of effective SSR missions and achieving the goal of implementation of SDG-16 targets. Therefore, there are many advantages of incorporating human security in making tighter connections between SSG/R and SDG-16.

CHAPTER 7

Analysis

This section analyses the strengths and weaknesses of human security in accounting for the linkages between SSG/R and SDG-16, and then concludes by making the argument that civilian oversight/accountability and participative approach/local ownership are crucial for making progress on the SDG-16 targets.

a. Strengths of human security as a bridge

There are numerous strengths of human security that enable it to serve as a bridge between SSG/R and SDG-16. Comprehensive, integrated, localized action is central for *Agenda 2030*, and human security would enable the accomplishment of these goals efficiently and effectively. Human security acknowledges that there are no one-size-fits-all solutions to problems. It emphasizes inclusivity, integrated and multidimensional attributes of response to threats to human survival, livelihood, and dignity (UNTFHS 2016). It would therefore significantly boost the effectiveness of SSR, which commonly emphasizes a more straightforward and technical approach in implementation (Dursun-Özkanca & Vandemoortele 2012). A major strength of the human security approach is that it focuses on 'tangible results at the local level of society,' which would significantly contribute to the attainment of the targets listed under SDG-16 (Grabek & Engwicht 2019: 2).

Human security looks at cross-cutting issues, such as threats to human life, livelihood, and dignity, and emphasizes different dimensions that are directly relevant to SDG-16 and SSR. For instance, personal security, political security, and community security are directly related to SDG-16 and SSR. It entails health, economic, food, and environmental security, too, which provides a greater connection between the security and development realms. It recognizes the multidimensionality of poverty and asserts that vulnerabilities must be tackled together. As aptly put by UNTFHS (2016: 13):

> By conceptualizing the relationship between the different components of the SDGs, the human security approach can frame future responses in a more interconnected and systematic fashion … [clarifying] how diverse issues interact and require mutually complementary solutions so as to ensure more sustainable and inclusive development.

How to cite this book chapter:
Dursun-Özkanca, O. 2021. *The Nexus Between Security Sector Governance/Reform and Sustainable Development Goal-16: An Examination of Conceptual Linkages and Policy Recommendations*. Pp. 47–53. London: Ubiquity Press. DOI: https://doi.org/10.5334/bcm.g. License: CC-BY-NC

Human security, just like SDG-16, is universal in its focus (UNGA 2013). SSR, on the other hand, is predominantly focused on post-conflict situations. Human security, through its context-specific as well as a universal approach, has the advantage of delivering better results on the SDG-16 targets. It deems that context-specific solutions reduce inequalities and promote inclusion. These ingredients help bind SSR better with SSG and SDG-16. Furthermore, human security holds that prevention is vital to avoid the negative impact of conflict and that early action is necessary to build resilience against conflict. As stated by the UNGA (2013: 4):

> [H]uman security initiatives promote solutions that identify the root causes underlying current and emerging threats, reveal possible mismatches between local and national as well as regional and international policies and programmes, and strengthen the capacities of Governments and people to reduce the impact of current challenges and prevent the occurrence of future crises.

In other words, human security's emphasis on context specificity ensures that action will take into account 'a more nuanced understanding of how different countries, districts within countries and groups of people experience the multidimensional aspects of poverty' (UNTFHS 2016: 12). The local factors receive extra attention from human security. As put by UNTFHS (2016: 12):

> By disaggregating social and economic indicators at the national and local levels, the human security approach is able to uncover the various factors that impede those who are most vulnerable, including women, minority groups and economically marginalized populations, from accessing essential public services and economic opportunities. Subsequently, services can be tailored to meet their specific needs. National and local priorities are established to advance an inclusive development process where the benefits of economic growth can reach the most marginalized and result in greater impact on the overall growth and social capital of respective communities.

Human security's multidimensional focus on both security and development can also benefit SSG/R, which do not necessarily place key importance on development. This is especially advantageous, as the SDGs bring together both security and development goals. Therefore, there is a need to link SSG/R more tightly to human security, in order to help achieve the targets of SDG-16.

None of today's challenges can indeed be resolved in isolation. Human security emphasizes the interconnectivity among today's problems. It therefore 'complements and enriches the mechanisms that will be needed in order to attain the SDGs' (UNTFHS 2016: 13). As the world strives to meet the SDGs in general and SDG-16 in particular, it is well advised to utilize human security's comparative advantage of promoting interconnected responses to cross-cutting problems. As the Commission on Human Security (2003: 2) has warned, the solution to such problems 'cannot be effective if it comes fragmented – from those dealing with rights, those with security, those with humanitarian concerns and those with development.' As the SDG-16 Conference (2019: 10) reaffirmed, 'Just, peaceful and inclusive societies can't be achieved if violence against children and women isn't tackled through a multi-sectoral and comprehensive approach.' This directly illustrates the strength and centrality of the human security approach in achieving SDG-16.

Furthermore, through its emphasis on a 'comprehensive approach to combating poverty and promoting sustainable development,' human security offers a 'practical approach for "why" and "how" the different parts of the United Nations system must come together to utilize their resources in a more integrated manner' (UNTFHS 2016: 12). In order to establish enduring peace, it is important to avoid the 'unintended consequences' of incoordination, when there are multiple international actors involved in peacebuilding (Dursun-Özkanca 2016: 50). Therefore, in order to successfully implement SDG-16, the stakeholders should emphasize the importance of human security's comprehensive approach. As the SDG-16 Conference (2019: 17) recommends, 'Interagency cooperation – particularly among public sector financial management, revenue authorities and authorities on anti-money laundering/combating the financing of terrorism (AML/CFT), as well as relevant small arms control authorities – should be strengthened.' It attracts attention to the existence of 'silos,' and argues that they 'are due in part to the failure to move beyond diversity to inclusion and non-discrimination' (SDG-16 Conference 2019: 17). 'Instead of breaking silos outright,' the SDG-16 Conference (2019: 17) recommends, 'teaching them how to dance together' as a long-term strategy. In this context, human security emerges as an important tool in the implementation of SDGs and SDG-16 in particular, to teach 'silos' 'how to dance together.'

Human security emphasizes a multi-stakeholder approach to complex problems. It brings together a broad range of stakeholders, to generate a more impactful and long-lasting outcome. The same is true for SDGs and SSG/R to a certain extent, albeit SSR has a long way to go to incorporate multi-stakeholders effectively into SSR missions, especially when it comes to local ownership. Human security has the advantage of 'guiding a more comprehensive and coordinated response by the international community to complex and multifaceted threats' (UNGA 2013: 9). A good example is Mongolia, where a comprehensive approach was pursued in response to the 'persistent poverty and recurring droughts' that adversely affected the well-being of isolated rural communities (UNGA 2013: 14). Several UN agencies along with national and local governments and civil society organizations worked collaboratively to successfully provide 'integrated support in the form of income-generating opportunities and access to information; improvements in sanitation and basic health-care services; and education and skills training' (UNGA 2013: 14). In Yemen too, the comprehensive approach of human security was put in action recently, as the UN collaborated with '254 humanitarian partners to agree on priorities and a coherent strategy to meet the needs of 13 million people' (UNGA 2019: 81).

Over the course of years, human security added a third pillar to its original pillars of freedom from fear and freedom from want: the freedom to live in dignity (UNTFHS 2016). It acknowledged the need to address problems at the personal, local, regional, and global levels simultaneously. It also called for responses to be preventive in nature. These are all attributes that are emphasized by SDG-16 as well as SSG/R.

Protection and empowerment lie at the heart of human security, just like they do in SDG-16 and SSG/R. 'As a people-centred, context-specific, comprehensive and prevention-oriented approach that advances both top-down protection and bottom-up empowerment solutions,' human security nicely complements SDG-16 (UNTFHS 2016: 11) and helps boost the power of SSG/R in facilitating the accomplishment of SDG-16. The goal is 'to empower the people to fend for themselves' and to enhance the livelihood of vulnerable people (The Commission on Human Security 2003: 6). In Timor-Leste, for instance, 'the establishment of community-based self-help groups was considered central to promoting an inclusive framework for reducing poverty, improving access to essential services and enhancing social inclusion,' illustrating the importance of people-centered and participative components of human security in a post-conflict setting (UNGA 2013: 12).

Moreover, it is important to discuss the 'do no harm' principle in this context. It is 'the minimum standard of practice to avoid causing inadvertent harm,' and seeks to 'understand the context,' 'understand the interaction between the intervention and the context,' and 'act upon that understanding in order to avoid negative impacts and maximize positive impacts on the conflict' (Conflict Prevention 2020). It acknowledges that 'aid is not neutral,' as 'aid and how it is administered can cause harm or can strengthen capacities for peace in the midst of conflict-affected communities … [due to] transfer of resources' (Conflict Prevention 2020). Therefore, 'the transfer of resources and the manner in which staff conduct the programmes can strengthen local capacities for peace, build on connectors that bring communities together, and reduce the divisions and sources of tensions that can lead to destructive conflict' (Conflict Prevention 2020). Applied to

SSG/R and SDG-16, 'do no harm' concept becomes a decisive factor in the success of institutional reform. For instance, critics have said that 'military assistance programmes of the donor countries in fragile states remain piecemeal and uncoordinated (in terms of training, doctrine and equipment procurement),' or assistance on DDR 'appear not to take enough account of specific conditions based in integrated economic, social and military analysis' (OECD 2010: 18). Human security's emphasis on the 'do no harm' principle would add an additional layer of protection by preventing unintended harm while conducting complex missions.

With regard to access to justice, the 'donor community should play a more active role in fragile states in raising awareness of individual rights and duties' (OECD 2010: 19). Nevertheless, it should be done by paying 'attention to how such campaigns affect social expectations, the balance of power and the political settlement underpinning the state' (OECD 2010: 19). Human security's context-specific approach along with its mantra of 'leaving no one behind' is instrumental in addressing these sizeable gaps in statebuilding, and admirably complement SSG/R and SDG-16 in creating stronger institutions that will take into account all citizens' interests.

Finally, the human security approach has been increasingly implemented since the end of the 1990s with much success. It has been applied to over 220 projects and programs under the direction of the UN Trust Fund for Human Security (UNTFHS) (UNTFHS 2016: 11). For instance, in March 2011, then UN Secretary-General Ban Ki-moon authorized for the formation of a task force, consisting of representatives from 'the Department for Peacekeeping Operations, the United Nations Development Programme (UNDP), the Department of Political Affairs, the Peacebuilding Support Office, the Office of the High Commissioner for Human Rights (OHCHR), the United Nations Children's Fund (UNICEF), UN Women and the World Bank' in order to 'integrate responses to transnational organized crime into the peacekeeping, peacebuilding, security and development activities of the United Nations, with [UN Office on Drugs and Crime] UNODC and the Department of Political Affairs as co-chairs' (UNODC 2012). This is referred to as the 'One-UN Approach,' and has 'improved coordination between stakeholders on organized crime networks and drugs trafficking' (Farr, Schnabel & Krupanski 2012: 337). As noted by UNTFHS (2016: 11), 'Through these initiatives, the added value of the human security approach in bolstering the operational effectiveness of the United Nations system and magnifying the impact of its work on the ground has been well documented.' As demonstrated in this section, human security offers numerous important comparative advantages in successfully achieving the SDG-16 targets while simultaneously contributing to the success of SSG/R.

b. Weaknesses of human security as a bridge

i. Narrow and broad definitions of human security

While human security's primary goal is the protection of human lives, there is some controversy as to what the individuals should be protected from and through what means (Shani 2007; Tadjbakhsh 2013). On this topic, there are those who favor a broad definition and those who prefer a narrow version of human security (Tadjbakhsh 2013: 43). The narrow understanding of the concept of human security argues that the international community should prioritize the insecurities and target military or physical threats to survival (Bueger & Vennesson 2009; Tadjbakhsh 2013). The broader understanding of the concept argues that the international community should expand the focus and include 'non-physical threats and injustice,' including economic inequalities, and lack of representation at political, social, and cultural levels (Bueger & Vennesson 2009: 18). As noted by Tadjbakhsh (2013: 44), the broader understanding of the concept consists of:

freedom from fear (conditions that allow individuals and groups protection from direct threats to their safety and physical integrity, including various forms of direct and indirect violence, intended or not); freedom from want (conditions that allow for protection of basic needs, quality of life, livelihoods and enhanced human welfare) and freedom from indignity (condition where individuals and groups are assured of the protection of their fundamental rights, allowed to make choices and take advantage of opportunities in their everyday lives).

While Japan led the way for the broader understanding of the concept, with an emphasis on 'freedom from want,' emphasizing the need to secure basic human needs with regards to food, economy, health, and environment, the Human Security Network, led by Canada, chose to focus on a narrower understanding of the concept by focusing on 'freedom from fear' from the use of force and violence (Burgess & Owen 2004). As such, one may make the argument that the broader understanding is focusing more on development, whereas the narrower interpretation of the concept is focusing more on security. The narrow approach 'may opt for policing strategies and humanitarian interventions to protect individuals in immediate danger' (Tadjbakhsh 2013: 49). Nevertheless, 'Restrictiveness would endanger the human security perspective of interconnection and is thereby less suitable as a perspective for research, mobilization, and civil society engagement – the way towards major long run impact' (Gasper 2010: 20).

Therefore, human security should 'remain flexible enough to allow for a deeper understanding of the root of insecurities and capacities to address them' (Tadjbakhsh 2013: 54). Many indicate that the broad approach requires long-term responses and prioritization (Oberleitner 2005; Tadjbakhsh 2013). For instance, Tadjbakhsh (2013: 48) argues, 'Dignity-related threats' should not 'be dealt with through short-term problem-solving approaches,' but require 'strategic planning, root cause analysis, [and] preventive action.' This paper makes a case that the narrow understanding alone does not provide a good bridge between SSG/R and SDG-16 and that the broader concept of human security is more suitable for the job at hand due to its focus on a long-term approach and emphasis on strategic planning.

As the SDGs have a 15-year timeline, a broader understanding of human security offers a more comprehensive and feasible alternative for meeting the targets of SDG-16. While it is true that the narrow understanding of human security is still found in some targets of SDG-16, such as Target 16.1 and Target 16.2, there are also many targets that seem to have embraced the broader understanding of human security. A broader understanding of human security would put SSG/R in a better position to help achieve SDG-16, as it would not only address short-term problems but also long-term challenges effectively. Otherwise, as indicated by an in-depth analysis of transitions from military to civilian power (Myanmar and Pakistan), transitions from 'war to peace' (Colombia, Sierra Leone), and transitions that resulted from independence (South Sudan) conducted by the UNDP and Oxford Policy Management, 'key challenges and weaknesses which remain unaddressed in moments of transition, risk becoming more entrenched structural problems' that 'are increasingly difficult to solve as time goes on' (UNDP & Oxford Policy Management 2019: 34).

Here, this manuscript makes the argument that the narrow understanding of human security mainly focuses on negative peace, whereas the broader understanding of human security also highlights positive peace. Negative peace mainly revolves around freedom from fear, as it emphasizes the absence of violence and war. On the other hand, freedom from want and freedom from indignity emphasize positive peace, as they seek to further integrate individuals into the society and create and sustain peaceful societies. Since SDG-16 contains both negative and positive peace targets, the broader understanding of human security is better situated to accomplish these targets overall.

ii. Actionability of the human security concept

Another criticism of human security is that it mainly focuses on principles rather than implementation (Paris 2001). With certain exceptions, the same argument may be made about SSG/R (Dursun-Özkanca & Vandemoortele 2012). Nevertheless, this does not mean that the focus on principles is inconsequential. As noted by Dursun-Özkanca and Vandemoortele (2012: 147), 'Like SSR, human security seeks a transformation of the way security is conceived.'

Like the SDGs in general, and SDG-16 in particular, the human security concept has been criticized as too ambiguous and difficult to implement. Paris, for instance, states that the human security concept is 'too vague to generate specific research questions' (Paris 2001: 93) and argues that it is mostly 'hot air' or 'empty rhetoric' (2001: 88). Paris (2001: 102) concludes that due to its vagueness, 'it verges on meaninglessness – and consequently offers little practical guidance to academics who might be interested in applying the concept, or to policymakers who must prioritize among competing policy goals.' Others indicate that empirical applications of human security are scarce (Ambrosetti 2008; Chandler 2008) and note that 'human security notions are often hard to apply in policy' (Gasper 2010: 19). Such critics add that this is due to 'problems concerning who cares and disagreements over who is responsible for action and who pays, reflecting the boundary-crossing character of the issues considered' (Gasper 2010: 19). Nevertheless, over the past decade, there have been an increasing number of studies that were conducted on the effectiveness of human security in delivering measurable outcomes, creating a 'second-generation human security' paradigm that focuses on operationalization and deepening of the ideas of individual security (Bell et al. 2013; Martin & Owen 2010; Newman 2016; Solar 2019; Werthes, Heaven, & Vollnhals 2011; Zeigermann 2020). Still, it has been criticized for producing some undesirable outcomes with regard to reconstruction of armed forces in a post-conventional war world (Solar 2019). There is still limited knowledge on 'how the institutional settings of international partnerships with conflict-affected states influence behavioural choices of households, firms, the international community, conflicting parties and elites; and how these affect broad development goals' (Zeigermann 2020).

iii. Human security and national sovereignty

While human security is typically based on idealist/liberal principles, the UNGA (2012) document emphasizes national sovereignty, due to concerns raised by UN member states on the Responsibility to Protect doctrine. UNGA (2012: 2) acknowledges that 'Governments retain the primary role and responsibility for ensuring the survival, livelihood and dignity of their citizens.' It adds, 'The role of the international community is to complement and provide the necessary support to Governments, upon their request,' and acknowledges 'that projects funded by the [UNTFHS] should receive the consent of the recipient State' (UNGA 2012: 2). While it is commendable that there is an emphasis on national ownership, these quotes may be interpreted as attributing key significance to the concept of national sovereignty vis-à-vis human security. As the historical data demonstrates, governments may conveniently forego the rights of their citizens, causing threats to citizens' well-being, survival, and dignity. Therefore, acknowledging that the role of the international community is simply to complement the governments may be interpreted as giving a blank check to some of the most atrocious governments around the world.

c. Implications of COVID-19 for human security

Finally, there are important changes taking place globally in the post-COVID-19 world order, ranging from 'nationalist deglobalization,' (increased nationalism paired with a process of uncoupling in the global economy) to less democratic participation, more centralization, the rise of a surveillance state, erosion of human rights, and to rising inequalities (Cooper & Aitchison 2020: 5). There is also the decline of multilateralism in global affairs and a 'fractured' liberal international order (Poast 2020), which may present further challenges for the comprehensive approach of human security and SSG/R to be successfully implemented to achieve SDG-16. As more and more countries are resorting to self-help and unilateralism rather than acting through international institutions, human security's prospects for successful implementation to accomplish SDG-16 decreases.

The COVID-19 pandemic similarly presents financial difficulties on fundraising efforts for the application of the human security approach to global problems. Fragile and weak states are expected to be disproportionately influenced by the COVID-19 pandemic 'due to their resource, infrastructure, and capacity deficits, but because of gaps in political legitimacy,' which, in turn, may exacerbate instability in such places over the long term (Graff 2020). The pandemic may also intensify the grievances that are already at the center of armed conflicts and lead 'authoritarian regimes prone to using government resources to suppress dissent' to step up these tactics and take advantage of the crisis to further consolidate power at the expense of civil society actors (Quirk 2020). Nationalism and populism are on the rise, making countries more volatile and prone to conflict. Therefore, it is even more essential to put a renewed emphasis on human security and the SDG-16-SSG/R nexus at this point in time.

CHAPTER 8

Next Steps: Policy Recommendations

SSG/R efforts must take account of economic issues, particularly the lack of employment opportunities for demobilized personnel as a result of DDR, and corruption's impact as a barrier against SSG/R as well as sustainable development. For instance, corruption has significant consequences for policy implementation and public service delivery (Hope 2020b). As such, SSG/R should go back to their development roots and better connect themselves with the sustainable development concept by operationalizing sustainable development goals as means for achieving better results in reforming the security and justice sectors. In doing so, SSR missions should put an increased emphasis on the buy-in factor for achieving the targets of SDG-16 from the whole population. Security sector actors should spend more time deliberating how to present the SSR initiatives in a way to create more popular support for such initiatives. Against this background, local ownership, participative approach, and legitimacy emerge as central concepts. The global trends in the post-COVID-19 world present an additional set of challenges for SSG/R as well as SDG-16. Consequently, democratic SSG acquires the utmost importance, and so do its vital components of oversight and accountability.

a. How can SSG/R help with SDG-16 targets?

This section addresses many ways SSG/R can help with SDG-16 targets, such as through promoting greater institutionalization and good governance principles, as well as its focus on reforming the security and justice institutions, by forming a closer connection between states and their populations. It may also help with its emphasis on good governance and capacity development (Hope 2020b). SSG/R may develop new tools to tackle transnational challenges and help achieve the targets entailed in SDG-16, especially through epistemic learning and sharing of good practices among epistemic communities around the world. For instance, SSG/R may enable national security sector actors to cooperate and jointly develop norms with regard to security provision or attainment of concrete targets listed in SDG-16. As noted in Resolution 2553 adopted by the

How to cite this book chapter:
Dursun-Özkanca, O. 2021. *The Nexus Between Security Sector Governance/Reform and Sustainable Development Goal-16: An Examination of Conceptual Linkages and Policy Recommendations.* Pp. 55–64. London: Ubiquity Press. DOI: https://doi.org/10.5334/bcm.h. License: CC-BY-NC

UNSC in December 2020, SSG and institutions 'can be enhanced through support to and inclusive national security dialogues; national security sector reviews and mappings; national security policy and strategy; national security legislation; national security sector plans; security sector public expenditure reviews; and national security oversight, management and coordination' (UNSC 2020b).

In order to achieve *Agenda 2030*'s goals, there is a need for a 'strong involvement of public service institutions,' including the ones operating under the framework of security and justice sector, and robust 'oversight mechanisms,' including NHRIs (DCAF, OSCE/ODIHR & UN Women 2019: 5). 'Institutional transformation in the oversight, management and services of security and justice sector institutions' emerge as critical for meeting the targets of the SDGs (DCAF, OSCE/ODIHR & UN Women 2019: 5). Therefore, in implementation, the human security concept should be linked to more operationalized policy tools under the framework of SSG/R and SDG-16. Otherwise, policies that rely on exclusion, discrimination, and inequality will prove to be significant roadblocks in achieving SDG-16 targets (DCAF, OSCE/ODIHR & UN Women 2019). Accordingly, drawing on the people-centered, inclusive, bottom-up, and context-specific attributes of human security, this section specifically focuses on oversight and accountability as well as participative approach and local ownership, noting that they hold the key for successful utilization of SSG/R's help in achieving the SDG-16 targets.

i. Oversight and accountability

This section focuses on the twin principles of oversight and accountability and examines how these concepts relate to SSG/R and SDG-16's different targets. It highlights their importance for resolving the problems SDG-16 is seeking to tackle. Oversight and accountability are among the basic tenets of democracies and ensure that defense, security, and intelligence actors are placed 'under a legal obligation to answer truly and completely the questions put to it by' the authorities to which it is accountable' (Hannah, O'Brien & Rathmell 2005: 12). After all, it is well established in the literature that recurring conflict and civil wars happen in countries 'where government elites are unaccountable to the public, where public does not participate in political life, and where information is not transparent' (Fearon 2011; Grant & Keohane 2005; Walter 2014: 1243). Thus, oversight and accountability are key elements to ensure peace and justice.

Oversight 'carries out "scrutiny" in the pursuit of efficiency, effectiveness and propriety,' and 'may take place before, during and after the fact' (Gill 2020: 4). It 'must be distinguished from "accountability" which requires officials to explain actions and to suffer the consequences or put the matter right if errors are made' (Gill 2020: 4). In that sense, as noted earlier in the report, oversight is a 'precondition for accountability' (Gill 2020: 4).

Accountability is the existence of 'clear expectations for security provision,' and as 'independent authorities oversee[ing] whether these expectations are met' (DCAF 2015: 3). If it is determined that such expectations are not met, then sanctions are imposed in order to remedy the situation (DCAF 2015). Alluding to the importance of oversight and accountability, the 2013 Report of the Secretary-General Ban Ki-moon (UNSG 2013: 5) notes:

> In all contexts, the United Nations is confronted by the need to ensure that it supports frameworks and interventions in the area of security sector reform that are inclusive and accountable, comply with human rights standards, and aim to enhance the social contract between the State and society and, ultimately, between the people and the security institutions empowered to protect them.

As made very clear by the former UN Secretary-General (UNSG 2013), accountability and oversight empower the people, by enabling them to hold the authorities responsible. In that sense, it is directly related to the concept of human security's people-centered view of security that highlights not only the provision of services such as protection but also empowerment. The focus on human security and freedom from fear prompted states to 'reorient security sector-related services from the imperative of external defence to the security of citizens and the upholding of their human rights' (Caparini & Cole 2008: 12). Due to its people-centered nature, human security holds that 'the provision of security should be directly responsive to the needs of the people,' allocating a significant role to be played by accountability and transparency (Caparini & Cole 2008: 16). Therefore, information should 'only be withheld [from ordinary citizens] for legitimate and tightly defined reasons' (Caparini & Cole 2008: 16). SSG/R similarly focus on the concepts of oversight and accountability, as they are basic principles of good governance. There is an increasing scholarly attention paid to public security programs that focus on 'safeguarding human rights and democratic freedoms, rather than "national" security' (Caparini & Cole 2008: 12).

There is also an increasing recognition of the linkages between human security, sustainable development, and SSG/R with particular attention to democratic control and accountability. For instance, in 2017, the European Parliament, the Council of the EU, and the European Commission adopted the *New European Consensus on Development: Our World, Our Dignity, Our Future*, recognizing the interlinkages between these concepts (Deneckere, Neat & Hauck 2020). The document was adopted in response to the UN's *2030 Agenda*. It acknowledges the mantra of the SDGs, 'leave no-one behind' and notes that the EU 'will implement a rights-based approach to development cooperation, encompassing all human rights,' and 'promote inclusion and participation, non-discrimination, equality and equity, transparency and accountability' (European Council 2017). Similarly, the 'bottom-up' SSR approach, which prioritizes 'smaller initiatives with immediate results,' such as human resources management, provides 'the means to build trust and long-term informal relations with change makers for political dialogue and … [paves] the way for longer-term engagements' (Deneckere, Neat & Hauck 2020: 31). Therefore, the bottom-up approach 'can have transformational effects in terms of making security institutions more accountable and more responsive to human security concerns' (Deneckere, Neat & Hauck 2020: 31).

As cautioned by many, in the security sector, 'excessive secrecy can be counter-productive' (Caparini & Cole 2008: 16; UK DFID 2002), as it may be 'used as a cover for financial mismanagement and illegal activities' (UK DFID 2002: 29). Ensuring accountability and oversight may contribute to the efforts to reverse 'the negative effects of "rent-seeking" (seeking income through positions of political power) and corruption on development' (Brzoska 2003: 14). Effective control of the security sector, and particularly the intelligence agencies, is important 'due to the inherent secrecy of their activities' (Hannah, O'Brien & Rathmell 2005: 12) and 'the secrecy laws [that] may hinder efforts to enhance transparency' (Fluri & Born 2003: 30). It ensures that security and intelligence actors do not act with impunity (Brzoska 2003). Oversight and accountability ensure that police, military, and intelligence agencies are 'serving the state as a whole rather than narrow political or other interests' (Gill 2020; Hannah, O'Brien & Rathmell 2005: vii), and that 'public funds are properly accounted for' (Hannah, O'Brien & Rathmell 2005: 12). They also ensure that security forces do not 'become agents of repression themselves, disregarding human rights' (Born, Buckland & McDermott 2014; Brzoska 2003: 30). Therefore, capacity development of oversight bodies, such as ombuds institutions, emerges as a central endeavor in SSR. Should they 'lack the independence, credibility, expertise and resources that are required,' they may 'fail to fulfil their mandates' (Born, Buckland & McDermott 2014: 4). Accomplishing this in SSR missions is easier said than done, as SSR support typically goes into train and equip missions. To illustrate, for the SSR mission in Mali, 'about 80% of international SSR support in the country' went into 'train and equip, while barely 20% of support cover[ed] accountability and governance aspects' (DCAF 2021).

Management and oversight of security and justice are conducted by state and non-state actors (Myrttinen 2019). State authorities include civilian administrative bodies like ministries of defense, interior, foreign affairs and finance, state oversight agencies like parliamentary bodies, ombudspersons, national human rights commissions, and the judiciary. Non-state actors that are involved in oversight include civil society organizations, academia, think tanks, and the media (Myrttinen 2019: 15). Accountability and oversight protect citizens from abuses and boost the ability of citizens to hold providers of security and justice accountable through increased responsiveness and enhanced accessibility to security and justice sector services. It, in turn, leads to greater 'confidence and legitimacy needed to overcome societal mistrust in violence-affected countries' (DCAF 2021).

Many studies have looked into the role of civil society, media, the legislative branch, and the executive branch in providing oversight of the police, military, and intelligence agencies and emphasized democratic policing and especially community policing principles, as well as democratic oversight principles (Caparini 2004; Caparini & Cole 2008; Hope 2020a). For capacity development to succeed, it should be an 'an endogenous process, supported by external actors' (Born, Buckland & McDermott 2014: 17). Some successful examples of the operationalization of oversight and accountability principles in SSR missions include the 'bottom-up accountability' concept implemented in Ecuador, leading to 'increased citizen participation in governance' through the 'citizen observatories known as Veedurias,' allowing citizens to monitor the implementation of the country's National Security Strategy and human security at different governance levels ranging from the municipal to national levels (DCAF 2021). Similarly, police-civilian partnerships may prove to be important for enhancing oversight and accountability in the security sector (United States Agency for International Development [USAID] 2020).

The importance of oversight and accountability becomes clearer in the context of newly democratizing countries. Democratization is often associated with a rise in political violence, as it often undermines the established privileges and raises political expectations that are not always or easily fulfilled (Luckham 2003). Furthermore, in newly democratizing countries, there may not necessarily be laws that guarantee freedom of access to information (Fluri & Born 2003). There may be tensions between oversight and efficiency of the security sector in post-transitional countries that recently made the switch from authoritarian to democratic regimes (Barany et al. 2019). Therefore, constitutional reform and SSR processes intersect in democratic transitions from military rule, civil war, and authoritarian regimes (Bisarya & Choudry 2020).

Moreover, the rising global military expenditures, deficiencies in the management of security services and the justice system, wasting of public resources through such deficiencies, violation of human rights by security providers and intelligence services, lack of access to information, underdeveloped civil society, security challenges in the aftermath of civil wars and conflicts, refugees and internally displaced people, inefficiencies in rehabilitating former combatants, lack of institutionalization, the proliferation of small arms and organized crime networks, and the rise of private military and security corporations all present different challenges for oversight and accountability. As Ball (2010: 41) notes, in SSR missions, 'All support should be based on the understanding that a security sector that is accountable to civil authorities and ordinary people is structured to meet security threats to individuals, their communities and their country.' Against this background, the importance of creating effective civilian oversight mechanisms as well as developing institutions to provide security is highlighted more (Ball et al. 2003).

To illustrate, one of the trends that have been identified in the SSR literature is the privatization of security (Portada, Riley & Gambone 2014; Richards & Smith 2007; Schultz & Yeung 2008). There are many private military and private security companies (PMSCs) that operate in the provision of internal and external security around the world, and they operate in a 'legal vacuum,' without much institutional framework that regulates their conduct (DCAF 2017; Tougas 2009: 322). Privatization of security calls for a more rigorous democratic oversight, as such organizations are not under the direct influence of governments. The Montreux Document as well as the

International Code of Conduct for Private Security Service Providers are steps in the right direction for the legal reforms to influence the PMSCs' 'operating practices in areas such as vetting, training and grievance procedures' (DCAF 2017: 12). Nevertheless, the UN Secretary-General's report in 2013 acknowledges that the UN does not 'as yet, see how best to acknowledge' these security institutions, and asks for a better understanding of 'their role in the provision of security' and in SSR (UNSG 2013: 5). It adds, 'The emerging trend towards the outsourcing to private companies of support to security sector reform introduces a new set of dynamics and challenges, including an increased need to ensure national ownership and democratic control and oversight' (UNSG 2013: 5).

The oversight of intelligence agencies may also present additional challenges due to lack of political will and the existence of asymmetric information (Gill 2020). Therefore, for oversight to be effective, there is a need for a 'clear statutory mandate, independence from the executive…, quality membership and adequate resources to employ expert staff, ability to maintain secrecy and thus gain trust of agencies and public, and political will to use powers in fulfilling mandate' (Gill 2020: 5). There is a 'trilemma' when it comes to oversight (Cayford, Pieters & Hijzen 2018: 1011): that is, it requires 'effectiveness, cost, and legality/proportionality', which is an 'impossible' task to 'successfully address all three elements' (Cayford, Pieters & Hijzen 2018: 1012). Such challenges are there not only for the newly democratized countries, but also for consolidated ones as well, presenting challenges for democratic SSG (Gill 2020).

SSG/R are based on an assumption that 'an ineffective and poorly governed security sector represents a decisive obstacle to peace, stability, poverty reduction, sustainable development, rule of law, good governance and the respect for human rights' and that 'responsible and accountable security forces reduce the risk of conflict' (Wulf 2011: 339). In that context, the human security concept's comparative advantage is heightened, as it holds a more multidimensional approach to interconnected problems. To illustrate, 'In the absence of democratic civilian control, security forces are able to act with impunity – with negative consequences for both human development and security' (Wulf 2011: 342). Therefore, over time, international donors have increasingly acknowledged the importance of security issues on development (Wulf 2011).

It is especially critical that beneficiary populations have means 'to hold donors accountable to their stated commitments to provide sustainable and effective development-sensitive SSR support' (Baldassini et al. 2018; Schnabel 2012: 64). In the same vein, donors should hold state authorities accountable to make sure that 'reforms are effectively implemented, and security and development objectives are met' (Baldassini et al. 2018; Schnabel 2012: 64). This is referred to as 'mutual accountability in SSR processes' (Schnabel 2012: 64).

Traditionally, parliaments have not received 'direct support through SSR programming in post-conflict and fragile contexts' (DCAF 2017: 7). But more recently, there has been some good progress made on 'the re-engagement of donors to strengthen the lawmaking and oversight functions over the security and justice sector,' which recognized the 'critical' role of parliaments in 'sustainable and accountable SSR processes' (DCAF 2017: 7). Consultations with people about their needs and expectations further enhance the legitimacy of the judicial and security institutions (DCAF 2017). Accordingly, citizen involvement, public participation, and engagement are important 'from the formulation and design to implementation, monitoring and evaluation phases' (SDG-16 Conference 2019: 4). On this point, human security can contribute significantly to ensure oversight and accountability by more actively involving the citizens in assessing whether SDG-16 is meeting its targets. Perceptions play an important role in assessing human security, which in turn has significant implications for meeting the SDG-16 targets. For instance, 'mainstreaming gender in SSR' by 'increasing gender awareness within the institutions' and 'empowering women and youth' are important 'in sustainable and effective prevention of conflict efforts' and in preventing 'gender-based violence' (DCAF 2017: 9).

Ensuring that 'the culture of impunity' is changed in security and justice institutions will be made possible through 'robust accountability mechanisms' that combine all 'three models of account-ability: internal, external by state institutions, and external by non-state institutions' (DCAF 2017: 10). As noted by DCAF (2017: 10), 'State level accountability is recognised as legitimate but may lack impartiality and often fails due to weak institutional capacity, cost implications, and the need for sustained political commitment to a culture of accountability.' Similarly, non-state alternatives involving the community and the media, 'can be cost effective, quick to put into place and accessi-ble, but may lack political clout, access and coherence' (DCAF 2017: 10). Finally, 'internal mecha-nisms can be an effective way of holding peers to account, but often lack transparency and public trust' (DCAF 2017: 10). Human security effectively fills these gaps in accountability mechanisms, as it emphasizes strong institutional mechanisms through the whole-of-government approach, the buy-in process and strategic coherence, and perceptions and people-centered perspectives.

Inadequate financing, 'misappropriation of funds, or poorly executed budgets' are among the reasons for 'poor performance of SSR processes, endemic corruption, and limited public confi-dence in the sector' (DCAF 2017: 11). 'Lack of salary payments' to security forces is a 'contribut-ing factor to low morale and ineffectiveness of security forces in a large number of post-conflict and fragile contexts, contributing to a lack of preventative capacity and often contributing to risks that security institutions become purveyors of insecurity' (DCAF 2017: 11). Therefore, effective management of public finances 'yielded positive results on the prevention of violent conflict' and 'boosted morale' among the officers in places such as Cote d'Ivoire, where before the reform defi-ciencies in salary payment caused 'repressive behavior of the military towards the population' (DCAF 2017: 11).

As put by the SDG-16 Conference (2019: 2), 'Corruption and mismanagement erode people's confidence in their governments. These must be resolved not just to deliver results but also to strengthen trust and promote stable societies.' 'Corruption, bribery, theft and tax evasion cost developing countries US$1.26 trillion per year' (UNDP Brussels 2017). As a result of successfully tackling corruption, funds could be effectively used in areas they are allocated to, further contrib-uting to sustainable development and institutional reform of the security sector.

SDG-16 delves into the 'core elements of a social compact between state and society' and seeks to guarantee 'a match between people's expectations of what the state and other actors will deliver … and the institutional capacity available within the state and other actors to meet those expectations' (UNDP 2016). It seeks to provide improved rule of law, a fair justice system, legal identity, safety, access to information, and opportunities for inclusion (UNDP 2016). Thus, accountable, responsive, and transparent institutions are of vital importance for achieving the targets of SDG-16 and to ensure the legitimacy of the security sector.

ii. Participative approach and local ownership

This section examines the concepts of participative approach and local ownership from the per-spective of both SSG/R and SDG-16 and emphasizes how these principles can help achieve better outcomes in SDG-16. As emphasized by the concept note published by the South African Presi-dency of the UNSC in December 2020, SSR's success is measured by its 'ability to deliver security and protection to diverse sections of the population and to serve as a basis for reconciliation through dialogue and the inclusion of local communities and their traditional security arrange-ments' (UNSC 2020a: 2). Similarly, many scholars attract attention to the contradictions between the practice of international trusteeship in post-conflict societies in the post-Cold War world and the concept of self-governance. They maintain that international statebuilding endeavors pose hurdles against a more organic form of government (Chandler 1999; Chesterman 2004; Knudsen & Laustsen 2006) and highlight the fallacies in the argument that liberal democracies are a solution to post-conflict peacebuilding (Newman, Paris & Richmond 2009). Liberal peacebuilding is criticized for its application of a standardized liberal model, which is deemed both insensitive to local contexts and disempower communities (Duffield 2010; Dursun-Özkanca 2018; Pugh, Cooper & Turner 2008; Richmond 2006). Further criticism holds that it has not so far achieved good results in terms of democratization and rule of law (Duffield 2010; Richmond 2006).

Others contend that liberal peacebuilding diverts the attention away from 'the realities of policy implementation' (Cubitt 2013: 112) and undermines the notion of local ownership (De Coning 2013). Cubitt (2013: 112), for instance, calls for the formation of 'more locally focused' models of democracy and economic restructuring by identifying 'the structures that work better … [and] local actors [that are] more dedicated to change.' De Coning (2013: 6) notes that because international actors believe that 'adopting neoliberal norms and institutions is ultimately in the best interest of the country in transition, some degree of coercion [from the outside and from the top-down] is justified.' Critics of liberal peacebuilding instead offer 'bottom-up' or 'local' approaches (De Coning 2013: 6; Dursun-Özkanca 2018).

Local ownership means that 'the reform of security policies, institutions, and activities in a given country … [are] designed, managed and implemented by domestic actors rather than external actors' (Nathan 2007: 9). Over the last decade, much has been written on local ownership (Donais 2008, 2009; Dursun-Özkanca 2018; Dursun-Özkanca &Vandemoortele 2012; Goodhand & Sedra 2010; Nathan 2007), yet its meaning is still disputed, as it means varying degrees of local control for different people (Chesterman 2007; Dursun-Özkanca 2018). Local ownership should be understood as both process – constantly updated during a mission to maximize local participation, and outcome – representing an exit strategy for international actors (Caplan 2006; Chesterman 2007; Dursun-Özkanca 2018; Dursun-Özkanca & Vandemoortele 2012; Hansen 2008; Mac Ginty 2015; Narten 2008; Nathan 2007). It is vital for the effectiveness, sustainability, and legitimacy of SSR missions (Edmunds, Juncos & Algar-Faria 2018; UNSC 2020a).

The concept of local ownership has its roots in the development circles that emphasized the importance of 'empowering local communities and encouraging local participation' in peacebuilding and democracy promotion (Dursun-Özkanca & Vandemoortele, 2012: 150). 'The language of ownership' was first used in OECD-DAC's *Development Partnerships in the New Global Context* document in May 1995 (Chesterman 2007: 7). The OECD endorsed the significance of promoting the local ownership in SSR missions back in 2001 (Dursun-Özkanca 2018). Then UN Secretary-General Kofi Annan referred to the concept in his report on exit strategies in UN peacekeeping missions the same year (UNSG 2001). Since then, the inclusion of local stakeholders, including government institutions, civil society organizations, and the wider public and local communities in the SSR processes emerged as a vital aspect in the evaluation of the success of SSR missions (Baker 2010; Ball 2010; Caparini 2010; Donais 2008; Dursun-Özkanca 2018; Dursun-Özkanca & Crossley-Frolick 2012; Dursun-Özkanca & Vandemoortele 2012; Nathan 2007; Simons 2012; Tholens 2012; Vandemoortele 2012). It is important for the missions to have people's support, inclusivity, representativeness, and legitimacy to ensure sustainability, local ownership, and successful SSR implementation (Dursun-Özkanca & Vandemoortele 2012; Hansen 2008; Law 2006; Nathan 2007; Schnabel 2012). Such missions should aim for 'transformative participation' rather than 'functional participation in order to gain 'buy-in,' minimise dissent (i.e., 'winning hearts and minds') and apply a veneer of local ownership' (Kunz & Valasek 2012: 131).

With regard to the implementation of the local ownership principle, SSR missions have mixed track records (Brzoska 2006). There is a gap in the literature on sources of local legitimacy in peacebuilding (Paris 2010), and on the lessons learned about local ownership (Dursun-Özkanca, 2014, 2018). Concepts of sustainability, proper implementation of reforms developed by outsiders, and the link between SSG/R and broader rule of law reforms are important dimensions of SSR as well as SDG-16.

Occasionally, sustainability and democratization as well as efficiency and efficacy of mission goals may clash in SSR missions (Dursun-Özkanca 2018). With regard to the efficiency of SSR missions, for instance, as it takes time and significant resources to engage in consultations with broad segments of the society, overlooking the local consultation process may prolong the duration of a mission and the presence of external actors (Blease & Qehaja 2014; Cubitt 2013; Dursun-Özkanca 2018; Gordon 2014; Narten 2008; Nathan 2007). A number of scholars draw attention to the fact that peacebuilding missions often fail to acknowledge the local political context and are generally conducted by excluding the non-elite members of local communities (Dursun-Özkanca 2018; Gordon 2014; Mac Ginty 2008; Papagianni 2009; Peake, Scheye & Hills 2006; Pugh, Cooper & Turner 2008). They warn that focusing solely on the local elites 'can undermine the extent to which SSR processes are broadly locally owned' by the local communities (Gordon 2014: 129). On that front, the inclusion of women and girls 'in institutional arrangements to guarantee their protection and full participation in peace processes' emerge as an important actionable item (UNSC 2020a: 3). The South African Presidency of the UNSC recently reiterated that the international community should focus on viable, sustainable SSG/R, called for 'bridging the gap between policy and practical implementation issues' on SSR, and advised the international community to use 'whole-of-mission strategies' that integrate national development plans and SSR (UNSC 2020a: 4–5). In Resolution 2553, which was recently adopted by the UNSC on SSR, the UN highlighted the 'centrality of national ownership', 'informed by the needs and aspirations of the entire population' for SSR processes (UNSC 2020b: 4).

Therefore, in order to ensure long-lasting peace, the local community's demands should be listened to and met (Chandler 2006). For instance, a key source of success behind the post-apartheid transformation of the defense sector of South Africa was its locally led and locally driven nature (DCAF 2021). Similarly, Community Safety Partnerships in Nigeria as well as the high level of local ownership in Senegal are successful implementations of the local ownership principle contributing to the success of SSR in these countries (DCAF 2021).

Accordingly, many believe that bottom-up approaches are more effective than top-down approaches to SSR because they emphasize the importance of the mission's sensitivity to the local context and the involvement of the local community in the reform process (Moore 2014). Others call for the application of indigenous practices in peacebuilding based on consensus decision making and compensation to ensure 'a grass-roots legitimacy' (Mac Ginty 2008: 155). Some warn, 'despite intentions to the contrary, donor-initiated SSR programmes tend to be primarily donor-driven, often with little input from beneficiaries at planning and implementation phases' (Schnabel 2012: 64). Martin (2012: 15) notes that the international community often sees local ownership 'as an impediment – an example of persistent misunderstanding, and often mistrust, between different groups.' However, SSR processes that do not take into consideration the local needs and demands and exclusively rely on the interest of external actors or domestic elites will have little resonance with the people at the community-level (Cubitt 2013; De Coning 2013; Hansen 2008; Martin 2012; Scheye 2008a, 2008b).

Therefore, 'the international community risks appearing hypocritical in emphasizing local ownership, when it is widely acknowledged that the involvement of local actors is significantly constrained' (Martin et al. 2012: 4). A good response to such criticisms of hypocrisy could be through ensuring 'local engagement' and participative approach, which could be more easily accomplished in countries 'where institutions are settled, [and] divisions of responsibility and chains of command are clear' (Edmunds, Juncos & Algar-Faria 2018: 234). Donors should relinquish 'a degree of control … in order to create the space and time for programmes to develop in their own dynamic and sometimes rather messy way' in order to 'give meaning to the aspirations for local empowerment' (Edmunds, Juncos & Algar-Faria 2018: 236).

Additionally, the SSR mission timeframes as well as the means and resources through which ownership is practiced emerge as important themes in discussions of local ownership

(Dursun-Özkanca 2018; Hansen 2008). In post-conflict peacebuilding missions, an important question emerges: When is the right time for the international community to withdraw from the field in a way to transfer power and responsibility to the local authorities? When the international community is predominantly concerned with efficiency in delivering the desired outcomes, local ownership may not be an attainable goal, given the time pressures that the missions operate under. In a similar vein, SSR 'processes are long-term endeavours that marry short-term crisis management tasks with the long-term development of institutions, capacity and culture' (Hansen 2008: 39). Therefore, a participative approach 'will have to be promoted across the entire spectrum of SSR activities to varying degrees and at varying stages' (Hansen 2008: 39). Time pressure may emerge as 'an excuse for bypassing local partners,' and concerns about security may 'override' the desires towards local ownership (Hansen 2008: 40). Under such circumstances, even though the international community retains some formal powers, 'its actual powers will be increasingly contested at the local level and will eventually wither away' (Peter 2013: 425).

For a successful implementation of SSR, an emphasis on SSG and 'a principled acceptance of democratic politics by the government, civil servants and security actors' are necessary (Wulf 2004: 9). The 'legacy of fragmentation, distrust and tension' in a post-conflict society 'makes it difficult to develop a rule-of-law culture and reach a local consensus on the form, purpose and priorities of the security architecture,' making the implementation of local ownership challenging (Dursun-Özkanca 2018; Hansen 2008: 41). Moreover, during democratization and in post-conflict and fragile states, justice and security are 'scarce commodities' (Scheye 2008b: 63), 'not only in terms of how they are provided but also to whom they are delivered and what objectives they are intended to achieve' (Wulf 2011: 349). 'Given that donor programming will inevitably create winners and losers, the important political question is local ownership by whom and for whom?' (Scheye 2008b: 63).

The concept of the social contract ascends in significance in countries affected by conflict, fragility, and fraught transition (McCandless 2020). As the UK DFID states in its *Building Peaceful States and Societies* and other documents, in order 'to rearticulate the linkages between state and society, strengthen the social contract, and foster legitimacy,' 'political settlements and political processes [should become] more inclusive by including not only the relevant actors to the violent conflict, but also incorporating other groups that have traditionally been excluded or marginalized' (Quoted in Rocha Menocal 2015: 7). When institutions are under the control of a narrow elite and display deeply personalized relationships, they are more prone to violent conflict than the ones that are more institutionalized and operate under the rule of law (North et al. 2009). 'Open access orders' allow for equality and inclusion, and channel opposition through the use of political processes that are available to the citizens (North et al. 2009: 2). The role of 'horizontal inequalities,' or exclusions based on group identity, cause state fragility and conflict, as they persist over time (Stewart 2008). The local ownership principle's application will determine whether 'populations [will] regard security services as being for them as opposed to being imposed from above or outside' (SDG-16 Conference 2019: 12). Context specificity and local ownership have also been acknowledged by SDG-17 and its Target 17.15 - 'Respect each country's policy space and leadership to establish and implement policies for poverty eradication and sustainable development.'

Accordingly, the local factors and the country-specific conditions have significant implications on the implementation of the local ownership principle in SSR (Dursun-Özkanca 2014). Local ownership, inclusivity, and representativeness of SSR missions are very much in line with the human security approach, which also emphasizes people-centered, context-specific, inclusive, and bottom-up engagement in complex problems. From the human security perspective, it is important to include the marginalized portions of the society in the SSR processes of decision making and implementation. Multi-stakeholder engagement is something that is also acknowledged by *Agenda 2030*. The goal behind stakeholder engagement in *Agenda 2030* is to ensure responsive, inclusive, participatory, and representative decision making at all levels of society. Emphasizing the 'leaving no one behind' principle, human security and SDG-16 ensures that 'those at risk of being overlooked have a voice in government decisions that affect them' (The Global Alliance 2019: 65). Furthermore, 'people-centered service delivery is critical to all the SDGs: from accessing education and health, to reducing inequality, to ensuring security, justice and the rule of law' (The Global Alliance 2019: 65).

Even though there is 'a growing awareness of the importance of incorporating local-level actors into peacebuilding and statebuilding processes, international actors have struggled to engage simultaneously both national-level actors and local communities' (Burt 2016: 2). As Burt (2016: 2) notes, 'SSR's contribution to SDG-16 and its targets will depend on the ability of programs to bridge the gaps' between the local, national, and international levels. SSR should, therefore, engage beyond the international-national level in order to contribute to state-society relations, 'which are at the core of peace and development, particularly in the fragile and conflict-affected states receiving SSR support' (Burt 2016: 2). On the topic, warning about the prospects of having an 'inclusive but not very participatory' multi-stakeholder consultations, the Global Alliance (2019: 66) notes:

> Although [formal consultative processes] may guarantee a few seats at the table to civil society representatives, often those participants are not very critical of the government. Moreover, such consultations often fail to incorporate civil society recommendations into policy efforts. It remains a challenge to ensure the participation of marginalized groups, especially when these embody overlapping marginalized attributes, such as women in indigenous populations.

Much lip service has been paid to incorporating views of the consumers and ultimate beneficiaries of justice and security services, that is, the local people, in SSR missions. Nevertheless, 'SSR assessments rarely take the time for local-level consultations,' due to the perception that it is 'a time-consuming, complex and costly activity' (Kunz & Valasek 2012: 131). If SSR turns 'its back on the lessons learnt regarding participatory development practices,' it is 'doomed to be a top-down, externally imposed process that fails to acknowledge the agency and authority of people who experience (in)security' (Kunz & Valasek 2012: 131). In assessing the success of SSR missions, it is important 'to take into account existing power dynamics and ensure that the voices of marginalised groups are heard' (Kunz & Valasek 2012: 137).

Therefore, human security's inclusivity, multidimensional and comprehensive approach, and its mantra of 'leaving no one behind' would be a good solution for the deficiencies identified in SSR missions in terms of the lack of local ownership and participative approaches. As a means to empower local people, 'SSR processes should move away from state-centrism to work with the full range of local-level security and justice providers, including women's organisations and customary authorities,' and incorporate 'formal and informal mechanisms for local-level collaboration between representatives of SSIs, customary authorities, community leaders and civil society groups' (Kunz & Valasek 2012: 137). As the *Pathways for Peace* document cautions, 'growth and poverty alleviation ... alone will not suffice to sustain peace' (UN & WB 2018: xviii), and there is a need for 'inclusive solutions through dialogue,' 'macroeconomic policies, institutional reform in core state functions, and redistributive policies' (UN & WB 2018: xix). In line with the comprehensive and multidimensional approach of human security, SSR needs 'to focus on more than just rule of law, and should include multi-sectoral approaches,' such as 'urban planning perspectives in terms of designing spaces that are perceived as functionally safe' (SDG-16 Conference 2019: 12). Therefore, participative and bottom-up approach and protection and empowerment principles of human security along with a renewed emphasis on local ownership provided by the SSR literature acquire a vital role in ensuring that SDG-16 targets are met.

Conclusion

Besides being goals in their own right, peace and good governance are 'also catalysts for achieving many other targets,' making SDG-16 central for the implementation of the overall *2030 Agenda* (SDG-16 Conference 2019: 2). Security and development are inextricably interconnected. No single actor, state or non-state, can tackle the complex development- and security-related challenges on its own. Civil wars and instability 'are often grounded in inequality, injustice and mismanagement of natural resources' (SDG-16 Conference 2019: 2). Compartmentalization serves neither the goal of achieving SDG-16 nor any other SDGs. Therefore, there is a need for a well-oiled cooperation machine at the international, national, and local levels.

SSG/R are critical for reforming the judicial and security sectors, the intelligence services, police force, correctional systems, and the military (Dursun-Özkanca & Crossley-Frolick 2012). In post-conflict settings, 'Stabilization and reconstruction are inextricably linked to security, governance, law and order,' making it 'vital that the new security infrastructures are carefully constructed, with special attention devoted to vetting, inter-ethnic balance in recruitment, and democratic oversight of the new security institutions' (Dursun-Özkanca & Crossley-Frolick 2012: 15). Building capacity in these sectors ensures the safety of the whole population (Meharg, Arnusch, & Cook Merrill 2010). Moreover, building democratically accountable and professional security forces is not only a critical component of peacebuilding efforts in post-conflict societies but also a key endeavor of SSG/R elsewhere (Dursun-Özkanca 2017; Dursun-Özkanca & Crossley-Frolick 2012). A holistic approach would significantly benefit SSR implementation (Dursun-Özkanca & Vandemoortele 2012), and human security would effectively contribute to it by using its comparative advantages of the comprehensive and multidimensional approach.

Human security lies at the heart of the nexus between UN's *Agenda 2030* and SSG/R and is important for creating a synergy between security and development in achieving common goals shared by SDG-16 and SSG/R. Cooperation and a holistic approach are necessary in order to tackle the increasingly complex problems that the global community faces, as illustrated by the ongoing pandemic. Since COVID-19 is a global problem that menaces all of humanity, global cooperation and 'global solutions' emerge as crucial elements of effective response to complex problems

How to cite this book chapter:
Dursun-Özkanca, O. 2021. *The Nexus Between Security Sector Governance/Reform and Sustainable Development Goal-16: An Examination of Conceptual Linkages and Policy Recommendations*. Pp. 65–68. London: Ubiquity Press. DOI: https://doi.org/10.5334/bcm.i. License: CC-BY-NC

intensified by the pandemic (UN 2020c: 11). Effective multilateralism has to be in place in order to successfully meet the SDG targets. Against this background, 'a whole-of-society approach' is needed with 'multidimensional, coordinated, swift and decisive' response (UN 2020c: 13). Human security ensures that a multi-stakeholder/comprehensive approach is in place.

This manuscript makes a case that while there are many commonalities between human security, SSG/R, and SDG-16, having a human security approach would ensure that these commonalities are weaved more tightly between SSG/R and SDG-16. SSG/R can help achieve SDG-16 by incorporating the guidelines provided by a broader understanding of human security that emphasizes both negative and positive peace. It further concludes human security's emphasis on reforming security and justice sectors and on accountability, oversight, and participative approach and local ownership can facilitate the accomplishment of SDG-16's primary objective of establishing peace, justice, and strong and inclusive institutions. Human security's 'leave no one behind' mantra would contribute to the institutional reform of the security and justice sectors by SSR.

This manuscript maintains that there is a need to link SSG/R with human security more closely, which in turn would ensure the fulfillment of SDG-16 targets more efficiently and effectively. Here it is important to remember that more often than not freedom from fear 'has its roots in freedom from want,' and 'addressing fragility, violence, and conflict is the only way for societies to develop' (Born 2018). Therefore, 'SSR efforts must take account of economic issues, particularly the lack of employment opportunities for demobilised young men and women' (Born 2018). In this context, combatting corruption should also be a top priority, as it has 'a catalytic effect on violence, and the perceptions of populations towards institutions at all levels can easily feed feelings of marginalization and exclusion' (SDG-16 Conference 2019: 12). Therefore, transparency, anti-corruption campaigns, and national human rights councils emerge as important efforts in SSR-SDG-16 linkage (SDG-16 Conference 2019).

Inclusivity is important for a successful implementation of SDG-16. Human security emphasizes inclusivity and the avoidance of exacerbation of inequalities. People-centered, context-specific, and nationally owned SSR can be made possible through the implementation of the human security approach. Furthermore, prevention-oriented SSR necessitates 'increasing the accountability, inclusiveness and resilience of the security sector within an institution-building framework' (Guerber 2018). Here, once again, SSR would benefit from integrating the inclusivity as well as the prevention-oriented approach of human security.

If there is one major observation that can be derived from the Black Lives Matter protests in the US and elsewhere in 2020, SSR and SDG-16 are not only developing world or Global South issues, but also Global North issues as well. The events following the murder of George Floyd while under police custody in Minneapolis emphasize the need to address SSR-SDG-16 linkages at a global level, rather than only at developing or post-conflict country levels. The inclusion of different voices, protection of the most vulnerable and marginalized people, a participative approach, equal access to justice, tackling corruption, and oversight and accountability are central to establishing tighter SSG/R-SDG-16 linkages.

The COVID-19 pandemic is not only a public health crisis but also is directly related to socio-economic development and poses challenges to peace, justice, international institutions, and global cooperation. This is a time of converging global crises, economic, health, racial, and systemic inequalities. The pandemic threatens the future capacity to meet the SDGs in general, and the targets of SDG-16 in particular. For instance, it could potentially 'reverse gains in gender equality and poverty alleviation in many countries' (Azcona et al. 2020: 1). Domestic and gender-based violence incidents have increased during the pandemic (Bettinger-Lopez & Bro 2020), hence, acquiring a better understanding of 'the gendered impact of this humanitarian crisis' is vital to 'guarantee the protection of all members of the affected population' (UN Women 2020: 7).

The global economy is shrinking due to COVID-19. The economic consequences of COVID-19 significantly increased governments' expenses around the world, 'plunging tax bases and a collapse of foreign exchange flows affecting, in particular, tourism-dependent countries and commodity exporters,' 'threatening the ability of many developing countries to service their external debts,' posing 'large risks for the attainment of the 2030 Agenda' (UN 2020b). While many countries around the world issued economic stimulus packages to minimize the negative impact of the crisis on their general population, the most fragile and the poorest countries in the Global South were unable to respond to the pandemic in an effective manner. The pandemic brought under the spotlight the unsustainable inequalities both within and between nations.

The implementation of the SDGs in general and SDG-16 in particular face additional hurdles due to the fact that financing of development will be acutely difficult. Conflict-affected and fragile countries, such as the G7+ countries, are struggling in responding to the pandemic. Lockdowns and closure of borders had the worst impact on conflict-ridden countries. Livelihood and well-being of immigrants and refugees are in danger. The crisis has the potential to reverse the gains made over the last couple of years towards accomplishing SDG-16 (#SDG16Plus 2020). International cooperation, multilateralism, and solidarity become more important in this context. G7+ issued a joint statement on the pandemic, calling for an immediate ceasefire to fight the virus, support for institutional learning at the peer-level (#SDG16Plus 2020).

The pandemic also brought to the forefront the systemic racism and violation of civil rights in many countries around the world. To illustrate, the pandemic was used as an excuse by some governments to curb freedoms of expression and other civil rights. This further highlights the importance of acquiring the human security approach and strengthening checks and balances in a way to give voice to all people. Good governance and strong institutions are also key in the context of the COVID-19 response and recovery with direct implications for the ability to advance the health and the well-being of citizens.

The pandemic is a complex problem requiring a comprehensive multilateral approach through global cooperation and global governance. SDG-16 is frequently viewed as a way to operationalize the global partnership aspect of SDG-17. International cooperation becomes more important in the post-COVID-19 world (Bernes et al. 2020). Multilateralism and solidarity can be a solution for inclusivity and interconnected problems (Khasanova 2020; Leal Filho et al. 2020; UN 2020c). In order to build resilience against global retrenchment, the countries around the world should create accountable, ethical, inclusive institutions at international, national, and local levels to ensure public trust. SDG-16's focus on transparency, accountability, and inclusivity calls for trust between the public and the government. This is necessary to address systemic issues. Participation and engagement of civil society is key to ensure effective and equitable response and provide oversight of governance response.

Partnerships between 'diverse actors' and diverse backgrounds 'from peace and security, to human rights to development' would also serve SSR well (Guerber 2018). It is also important to 'strengthen the comprehensive, integrated, and coherent approach' of the UN in SSR and improve its 'strategic partnerships' with 'regional and subregional arrangements and organizations,' such as the African Union in order to 'foster strategic coherence of efforts' (UNSC 2020b: 7–8). Therefore, the multi-stakeholder and comprehensive approach of human security would help SSR to accomplish different targets of SDG-16. We should put human security, SSG/R, and SDG-16 at the heart of the COVID-19 response and recovery, in order to ensure that the pandemic response does not divert the world's attention away from founding peaceful societies, establishing justice, and providing transparency so that public trust and inclusive policies are part of recovery planning and implementation.

Finally, while timelines are good for pressuring member states to accomplish the goals by a certain deadline, they may also lead to certain tasks not being fulfilled completely, causing them to focus on short-term gains that are easily assessable rather than longer-term goals that are harder to achieve and assess. In that sense, the SDG timeline of 2030 may lead stakeholders to focus on making progress on negative peace targets rather than on positive peace targets, as the former are easier to assess and accomplish when compared to the latter. To illustrate, tracking progress on negative peace items such as Target 16.1 on violence reduction is easier and more straight-forward, when compared to assessing positive peace items such as Target 16.6 on transparency and accountability or Target 16.7 on inclusiveness in participation, essential good governance principles. Since international institutions are interested in proving their success through assess-able goals, they may be inclined to lower the bar for expectations for peace, justice, and strong institutions to save face.

All in all, a concurrent emphasis on security and development is needed for addressing the issues under the purview of SDG-16. The political will to stay on course and fully achieve both negative and positive peace targets as well as long-term funding emerge as important factors, as do coordination and cooperation between different stakeholders. As demonstrated in this mansu-cript, SSG/R and human security have a promising potential to ensure that the SDGs, particularly SDG-16, will not face the fate of the MDGs.

References

Ahmed, F, Ahmed, N, Pissiarides, C and **Stiglitz, J** 2020 Why inequality could spread COVID-19. *The Lancet Public Health,* 5(5): e240.

Allen, C, Metternicht, G and **Wiedmann, T** 2018 Prioritising SDG targets: Assessing baselines, gaps and interlinkages. *Sustainability Science,* 14(2): 421–438. DOI: https://doi.org/10.1007/s11625-018-0596-81.

Ambrosetti, D 2008 Human security as political resource: A response to David Chandler's 'human security: The dog that didn't bark.' *Security Dialogue,* 39(4): 439–444.

Andrimihaja, N A, Cinyabuguma, M and **Devarajan S** 2011 Avoiding the fragility trap in Africa. *World Bank Africa Region Policy Research Working Paper,* 5884, November.

Athorpe, R 1997 Some relief from development: Humanitarian emergency aid in the Horn of Africa (including Sudan), Rwanda and Liberia. *The European Journal of Development Research,* 9(2): 83–106.

Azcona, G, Bhatt, A, Davies, S, Harman, S, Smith, J and **Wenham, C** 2020 Spotlight on gender, COVID-19 and the SDGs: Will the pandemic derail hard-won progress on gender equality? *UN Women Spotlight on the SDGs Series.* New York: UN Women.

Baker, B 2010 The future is non-state. In: Sedra, M (Ed.) *The Future of Security Sector Reform.* Waterloo, ON: The Centre for International Governance Innovation [CIGI]. pp. 208–228.

Baldassini, E, Dyk, R, Krupanski, M, Meibauer, G, Schnabel, A, Trepp U and **Zumsteg, R** 2018 Tracking the development dividend of SSR: Research report. Project supported by the Folke Bernadotte Academy (FBA) and the Geneva Centre for the Democratic Control of Armed Forces (DCAF), February. Available at: https://www.dcaf.ch/sites/default/files/publications/documents/Tracking%20the%20Development%20Dividend%20of%20SSR_18Feb2018.pdf [Last accessed 15 February 2021].

Ball, N and **Hendrickson D** 2009 Trends in security sector reform: Policy, practice, research. *CSDG Papers* 20.

Ball, N 2010 The evolution of the security sector reform agenda. In: Sedra, M (Ed.) *The Future of Security Sector Reform.* Waterloo, ON: CIGI. pp. 29–44.

Ball, N, Fayemi, J K, Olonisakin, F and **Williams, R** with **Rupia M** 2003 Governance in the security sector. In: van de Walle, N and Ball, N (eds.) *Beyond Structural Adjustment.* New York: Palgrave. pp. 263–304.

Barany, Z, Bisarya, S, Choudhry, S, and **Stacey, R** (eds.) 2019 *Security Sector Reform in Constitutional Transitions.* London: Oxford University Press.

Barbier, E B and **Burgess, J C** 2020 Sustainability and development after COVID-19. *World Development*, 135(November): 105082.

Bell, S R, Murdie, A, Blocksome, P, and **Brown, K** 2013 'Force multipliers': Conditional effectiveness of military and INGO human security interventions. *Journal of Human Rights*, 12(4): 397–422.

Benner, T and **Rotmann, P** 2008 Learning to learn? UN peacebuilding and the challenges of building a learning organization. *Journal of Intervention and Statebuilding*, 2(1): 43–62.

Berg, V and **Varsori, A** 2020 COVID-19 is increasing the power of Brazil's criminal groups. *LSE Latin America and Caribbean Blog*, 28 May. Available at: http://eprints.lse.ac.uk/104860/ [Last accessed 15 February 2021].

Bergenas, J and **Mahoney, G** 2016 SDG-16: A platform for a new era of international cooperation. *Impakter.com SDG Series*, 2 August. Available at: https://impakter.com/SDG-16-platform-new -era-international-cooperation/#comments [Last accessed 15 February 2021].

Bernes, T, Brozus, L, Hatuel-Radoshitzky, M, Heistein, A, Greco, E, Sasnal, P, Yurgens, I, Kulik, S, Turianskyi, Y, Gruzd, S, Sidiropoulos, E, Grobbelaar, N, Yenel, S, Regazzoni, C J, Dongxiao, C, Chuanying, L, Kapur, K, Suri, S, Vermonte, P, Damuri, Y R, Muhibat, S, and **Caballero-Anthony, M** 2020 Challenges of global governance amid the COVID-19 pandemic. Council on Foreign Relations International Institutions and Global Governance Program Paper Series, May. Available at: https://cdn.cfr.org/sites/default/files/report_pdf/challenges-of -global-governance-amid-the-covid-19-pandemic.pdf [Last accessed 15 February 2021].

Bettinger-Lopez, C and **Bro, A** 2020 A double pandemic: Domestic violence in the age of COVID-19. *Council on Foreign Relations*, In Brief, 13 May. Available at: https://www.cfr.org /in-brief/double-pandemic-domestic-violence-age-covid-19 [Last accessed 15 February 2021].

Bisarya, S and **Choudhry, S** 2020 Security sector reform in constitutional transitions. *International IDEA Policy Paper* No. 23. Stockholm: International IDEA.

Bisca P M 2018 Development for security: Lending for peace? *Brookings Future Development*, 20 April. Available at: https://www.brookings.edu/blog/future-development/2018/04/20/develop ment-for-security-lending-for-peace/ [Last accessed 15 February 2021].

Blease, D and **Qehaja, F** 2013 The conundrum of local ownership in developing a security sector: The case of Kosovo. *New Balkan Politics*, 14: 1–21.

Blind, P K 2019 Humanitarian SDGs: Interlinking the 2030 Agenda for Sustainable Development with the agenda for humanity. *DESA Working Paper* No. 160, ST/ESA/2019/DWP/160, May. Available at: https://www.un.org/esa/desa/papers/2019/wp160_2019.pdf [Last accessed 15 February 2021].

Born, H 2018 Security sector reform as a tool for development. *PASS*, 6 November. Available at: https://www.pass-usa.net/security-sector-reform-as-a-tool-for-development [Last accessed 15 February 2021].

Bouris, D 2012 The European Union's role in the Palestinian Territories: State-building through security sector reform? *European Security*, 21(2): 257–271.

Bousquet, F 2019 Humanitarian-development-peace partnerships: Aligning to tackle fragility, conflict and violence. *World Bank Blogs*, 22 July. Available at: https://blogs.worldbank.org /voices/humanitarian-development-peace-partnerships-aligning-tackle-fragility-conflict -and-violence [Last accessed 15 February 2021].

Boyce, J K 2002 Investing in peace: Aid and conditionality after civil wars. *Adelphi Paper*, 351. New York: Oxford University Press.

Brikci, N, and **Holder, A** 2011 MDG4: Hope or despair for Africa? *Revista De Economia Mundial*, 27: 71–94.

Brown, S 2011 Aid effectiveness and the framing of new Canadian aid initiatives. In: Bratt D and Kukucha C J (eds.), *Readings in Canadian Foreign Policy: Classic Debates and New Ideas*, Toronto: Oxford University Press. pp. 469–486.

Bruneau, T and **Matei, F** 2008 Towards a new conceptualization of democratization and civil-military relations. *Democratization*, 15(5): 909–929.

Brzoska, M 2000 The concept of security sector reform. *Bonn International Centre for Conversion Brief*, 15(June): 6–13.

Brzoska, M 2003 Development donors and the concept of security sector reform. DCAF Occasional Paper, 4(November). Geneva: DCAF.

Brzoska, M 2006 Introduction: Criteria for evaluating post-conflict reconstruction and security sector reform in peace support operations. *International Peacekeeping*, 13(1): 1–13. DOI: https://doi.org/10.1080/13533310500424603.

Bueger, C and **Vennesson, P** 2009 Security, development and the EU's development policy. *European Union Institute Working Paper*, June. Available at: https://core.ac.uk/download/pdf/45687972.pdf [Last accessed 15 February 2021].

Burgess, J P and **Owen, T** (eds.) 2004 Special section on what is human security? *Security Dialogue* 35(3): 345–387.

Born, H, Buckland, B S and **McDermott, W** 2014 *Capacity Development and Ombuds Institutions for the Armed Forces.* Geneva: DCAF.

Burt, G 2016 Security sector reform, legitimate politics and SDG-16. *Centre for Security Governance SSR 2.0 Brief*, 5(July). Available at: https://secgovcentre.org/wp-content/uploads/2016/11/SSR-2.0-Brief-5_-_Burt_-_July_2016.pdf [Last accessed 15 February 2021].

Bryden, A 2007 From policy to practice: Gauging the OECD's evolving role in security sector reform. In: Law, D M (ed.), *Intergovernmental Organizations and Security Sector Reform.* Geneva: DCAF. pp. 65–84.

Caparini, M 2003 Security sector reform and NATO and EU enlargement. In: Hänggi, H and Winkler, T (eds.), *Challenges of security sector governance.* Geneva: DCAF. pp. 237–260.

Caparini M 2004 Civil society and democratic oversight of the security sector: A preliminary investigation. In: Fluri, P and Hadžić, M (eds.) *Sourcebook on Security Sector Reform: Collection of Papers.* Geneva: DCAF. pp. 171–192.

Caparini, M 2010 Civil society and the future of security sector reform. In: Sedra, M (ed.), *The Future of Security Sector Reform.* Waterloo, ON: CIGI. pp. 244–262.

Caparini, M and **Cole, E** 2008 The case for public oversight of the security sector: Concepts and strategies. In: Cole, E, Eppert, K, and Kinzelbach, K (eds.) *Public Oversight of the Security Sector: A Handbook for Civil Society Organizations.* Geneva: DCAF and UNDP. pp. 11–30.

Caplan, R 2005 *International Governance of War-Torn Territories: Rule and Reconstruction.* Oxford: Oxford University Press.

Caplan, R 2006 After exit: Successor missions and peace consolidation. *Civil Wars*, 8 (3–4): 253–267.

Cayford, M, Pieters, W, and **Hijzen, C** 2018 Plots, murders, and money: Oversight bodies evaluating the effectiveness of surveillance technology. *Intelligence and National Security*, 33(7): 999–1021.

Centre for Integrity in the Defence Sector 2014 *Integrity action plan: A handbook for practitioners in defence establishments.* Available at: https://cids.no/wp-content/uploads/2014/12/Integrity-Action-Plan-handbook_web.pdf [Last accessed 15 February 2021].

Chanaa, J 2002 *Security Sector Reform: Issues, Challenges and Prospects.* Oxford: Oxford University Press.

Chandler, D 1999 *Bosnia: Faking Democracy After Dayton.* London: Pluto.

Chandler, D 2006 Back to the future? The limits of neo-Wilsonian ideals of exporting democracy. *Review of International Studies*, 32(3): 475–494.

Chandler, D 2008 Human security: The dog that didn't bark. *Security Dialogue*, 39(4): 427–438.

Chesterman, S 2004 *You the People: The United Nations, Transitional Administration, and State.* New York: Oxford University Press.

Chesterman, S 2007 Ownership in theory and practice: Transfer of authority in UN statebuilding operations. *Journal of Intervention and Statebuilding*, 1(1): 3–26.

Chuter, D 2006 Understanding security sector reform. *Journal of Security Sector Management*, 4(2): 1–21.

Collier, P 1999 On the economic consequences of civil war. *Oxford Economic Papers*, 51(1): 168–183.

Collier, P and **Hoeffler, A** 2004 Greed and grievance in civil war. *Oxford Economic Papers*, 56(4): 563–595.

Collinson, S, Elhawary S, and **Muggah, R** 2010 States of fragility: Stabilisation and its implications for humanitarian action. *Humanitarian Policy Group Working Paper*, Oversees Development Institute, May. Available at: https://www.odi.org/sites/odi.org.uk/files/odi-assets/publications -opinion-files/5978.pdf [Last accessed 15 February 2021].

Commission on Human Security 2003 *Human Security Now.* New York. Available at: https: //reliefweb.int/sites/reliefweb.int/files/resources/91BAEEDBA50C6907C1256D19006A9353 -chs-security-may03.pdf [Last accessed 15 February 2021].

Conflict Prevention 2020 Do no harm. Available at: https://conflictsensitivity.org/conflict-sensi tivity/do-no-harm-local-capacities-for-peace-project/ [Last accessed 15 February 2021].

Connecticut Law Tribune Editorial Board 2020 Anonymous, unaccountable police must not be tolerated in our society. 6 August. Available at: https://www.law.com/ctlawtribune /2020/08/06/anonymous-unaccountable-police-must-not-be-tolerated-in-our-society/?slreturn =20200816130828 [Last accessed 12 September 2020].

Cooper, L and **Aitchison, G** 2020 Covid-19, authoritarianism and democracy. LSE Conflict and Civil Society Research Unit, June. Available at: http://eprints.lse.ac.uk/105103/4/dangers _ahead.pdf [Last accessed 15 February 2021].

Council of Europe 2018 Paris principles at 25: Strong national human rights institutions needed more than ever, 18 December. Available at: https://www.coe.int/en/web/commissioner/-/paris -principles-at-25-strong-national-human-rights-institutions-needed-more-than-ever [Last accessed 15 February 2021].

Council of the European Union 2003 A secure Europe in a better world: European security strat- egy. Brussels, 12 December. Available at: http://www.consilium.europa.eu/uedocs/cmsUpload /78367.pdf [Last accessed 15 February 2021].

Council of the European Union 2005 EU concept for ESDP support to security sector reform (SSR). Brussels, 13 October, 12566/4/05.

Cramer, C 2003 Does inequality cause conflict? *Journal of International Development*, 15(4): 397–412.

Crossley-Frolick, K and **Dursun-Özkanca, O** 2012 Security sector reform and transitional jus- tice in Kosovo: Comparing the Kosovo Security Force and Police Reform Processes. *Journal of Intervention and Statebuilding*, 6(2): 121–143.

Cubitt, C 2013 Responsible reconstruction after war: Meeting local needs for building peace. *Review of International Studies*, 39(1): 91–112.

De Coning, C 2013 Understanding peacebuilding as essentially local. *Stability: International Jour- nal of Security and Development*, 2(1): 1–6.

Deneckere, M, Neat, A and **Hauck, V** 2020 The future of EU security sector assistance: Learn- ing from experience. *ECDPM Discussion Paper*, 271, May. Available at: https://ecdpm.org /wp-content/uploads/ECDPM-Future-EU-Security-Sector-Assistance-Learning-Experience -Discussion-Paper-271.pdf [Last accessed 15 February 2021].

Development Initiatives 2017 *ODA Modernisation: Background Paper.* September. Available at: http://devinit.org/wp-content/uploads/2017/09/Backgound-paper_ODA-modernisation.pdf [Last accessed 15 February 2021].

Dodds, F and **Bartram, J** (eds.) 2016 *The Water, Food, Energy and Climate Nexus: Challenges and An Agenda for Action.* New York: Routledge.

Doelle, P and **de Harven, A G** 2008 Security sector reform: A challenging concept at the nexus between security and development. In: Spence, D and Fluri, P (eds.) *The European Union and Security Sector Reform.* London: John Harper Publishing. pp. 38–51.

Donais, T (ed.) 2008 *Local Ownership and Security Sector Reform.* Geneva: DCAF. Available at: http://www.dcaf.ch/Publications/Local-Ownership-and-Security-Sector-Reform [Last accessed 15 February 2021].

Donais, T 2009 Empowerment or imposition? Dilemmas of local ownership in post-conflict peacebuilding processes. *Peace and Change,* 34(1): 3–26.

Donais, T and **McCandless, E** 2016 International peace building and the emerging inclusivity norm. *Third World Quarterly,* 38(2): 291–310.

Duffield, M 2001 *Global Governance and the New Wars: The Merging of Development and Security.* London: Zed Books.

Duffield, M 2007 *Development, Security and Unending War: Governing the World of Peoples.* Cambridge: Polity.

Duffield, M 2010 The liberal way of development and the development-security impasse: Exploring the global life-chance divide. *Security Dialogue,* 41(1): 53–76.

Durojave, E 2010 Corruption as a threat to human security in Africa. In: Abbas, A (ed.) *Protecting Human Security in Africa.* London: Oxford University Press. Chapter 10.

Dursun-Özkanca, O (ed.) 2014 *The European Union as An Actor in Security Sector Reform: Current Practices and Challenges of Implementation.* New York: Routledge.

Dursun-Özkanca, O 2016 The assembly-line model of peacebuilding: Towards a theory of international collaboration in multidimensional peacebuilding operations. *International Journal of Peace Studies,* 21(2): 41–57.

Dursun-Özkanca, O 2017 Pitfalls of police reform in Costa Rica: Insights into security sector reform in non-military countries. *Peacebuilding* 5(3): 320–338.

Dursun-Özkanca, O 2018 The European Union Rule of Law Mission in Kosovo: An analysis from the local perspective. *Ethnopolitics,* 17(1): 71–94.

Dursun-Özkanca, O and **Crossley-Frolick, K A** 2012 Security sector reform in Kosovo: The complex division of labour between the EU and other multilateral institutions in building Kosovo's police force. *European Security,* 21(2): 236–256.

Dursun-Özkanca, O and **Vandemoortele, A** 2012 The European Union and security sector reform: Current practices and challenges of implementation. *European Security,* 21(2): 139–160.

Easterly, W 2009 How the millennium development goals are unfair to Africa. *World development,* 37(1): 26–35.

Economic and Social Council (ECOSOC) 2020. Draft ministerial declaration of the high-level segment of the 2020 session of the Economic and Social Council and the 2020 high-level political forum on sustainable development, convened under the auspices of the Council, on the theme 'Accelerated action and transformative pathways: realizing the decade of action and delivery for sustainable development,' 17 July, E/2020/L.20-E/HLPF/2020/L.1.

Economist Intelligence Unit 2020 *Down but not Out? Globalisation and the Threat of Covid-19.* Report, June.

Edmunds, T 2007 *Security Sector Reform in Transforming Societies: Croatia, Serbia, Montenegro.* Manchester: Manchester University Press.

Edmunds, T, Juncos, A E and **Algar-Faria, G** 2018 EU local capacity building: Ownership, complexity and agency. *Global Affairs,* 4(2–3): 227–239.

European Commission 2019 African Peace Facility: African Union peace & security operations boosted by an additional €800 million from the European Union. Press Release,

22 July. Available at: https://ec.europa.eu/commission/presscorner/detail/en/IP_19_3432 [Last accessed 15 February 2021].

European Council 2017 *The New European Consensus on Development: 'Our World, Our Dignity, Our Future.'* Joint statement by the Council and the representatives of the government of the member states meeting within the Council, the European Parliament and the European Commission, June 26. Available at: https://op.europa.eu/en/publication-detail/-/publication/5a95e892-ec76-11e8-b690-01aa75ed71a1 [Last accessed 15 February 2021].

European External Action Service (EEAS) 2019 The European Union's global strategy three years on, looking forward, June.

European External Action Service (EEAS) 2016 A global strategy for the European Union's Foreign and Security Policy. Shared Vision, Common Action: A Stronger Europe, June.

Evans, W 2012 A review of the evidence informing DFID's 'Building Peaceful States and Societies' practice paper. *Paper 1: Political Settlements, Peace Settlements, and Inclusion.* London: DFID.

Faleg, G 2012 Between knowledge and power: Epistemic communities and the emergence of security sector reform in the EU security architecture. *European Security*, 21(2): 161–184.

Farr, V, Schnabel, A and **Krupanski, M** 2012 It takes two to tango: Towards integrated development and SSR assistance. In: Schnabel, A and Farr, V (eds.) *Back to the Roots: Security Sector Reform and Development.* Münster: LIT Verlag. pp. 321–342.

Fearon, J D 2011 Governance and civil war onset. *World Development Report 2011.* Background Paper. Washington, DC: World Bank.

Fehling, M, Nelson, B D, and **Venkatapuram, B** 2013 Limitations of the Millennium Development Goals: A literature review. *Global Public Health*, 8(10): 1109–1122. DOI: https://doi.org/10.1080/17441692.2013.845676.

Ferreiro, M 2012 Blurring of lines in complex emergencies: Consequences for the humanitarian community. *The Journal of Humanitarian Assistance*, 24 December. Available at: http://sites.tufts.edu/jha/archives/1625 [Last accessed 15 February 2021].

Fitz-Gerald, A M 2012 Lest we forget? The centrality of development considerations in internationally assisted SSR processes. In: Schnabel, A and Farr, V (eds.), *Back to the Roots: Security Sector Reform and Development.* Münster: LIT Verlag. pp. 293–320.

Fluri, P and **Born, H** (eds.) 2003 *Parliamentary Oversight of the Security Sector: Principles, Mechanisms and Practices.* Geneva: DCAF.

Fukuda-Parr, S 2010 Reducing inequality – The missing MDG: A content review of PRSPs and bilateral donor policy statements. *Institute of Development Studies Bulletin*, 41(1): 26–35. DOI: https://doi.org/10.1111/j.1759-5436.2010.00100.x.

Gaile G L and **Ferguson A** 1996 Success in African social development: Some positive indications. *Third World Quarterly*, 17(3): 557–572.

Galtung, J 1964 A structural theory of aggression. *Journal of Peace Research*, 1(2), 95–119.

Gasper, D R 2010 The idea of human security. *ISS Staff Group 2: States, Societies and World Development.* Cambridge University Press. Available at: http://hdl.handle.net/1765/22373 [Last accessed 15 February 2021].

Geneva Centre for the Democratic Control of Armed Forces (DCAF) 2021 Balancing accountability and effectiveness. *Principles in Practice.* Available at: https://issat.dcaf.ch/Learn/SSR-in-Practice/Principles-in-Practice/Balancing-Accountability-and-Effectiveness [Last accessed 15 February 2021].

Geneva Centre for the Democratic Control of Armed Forces (DCAF) 2015 Security sector governance. SSR Backgrounder Series (Geneva: DCAF).

Geneva Centre for the Democratic Control of Armed Forces (DCAF) 2017 The contribution and role of SSR in the prevention of violent conflict. Report, July, Geneva: DCAF. Available at:

https://issat.dcaf.ch/download/115130/2101437/SSR%20contribution%20to%20Preventing %20Violent%20Conflict%202017_Final.pdf [Last accessed 15 February 2021].

Geneva Centre for the Democratic Control of Armed Forces (DCAF), OSCE/ODIHR and **UN Women** 2019 The 2030 Agenda for sustainable development, the security sector and gender equality. Policy Brief. Gender and Security Toolkit. Geneva: DCAF, OSCE/ODIHR, UN Women. Available at: https://www.dcaf.ch/sites/default/files/publications/documents /GSPolicyBrief_4%20EN%20FINAL_1.pdf [Last accessed 15 February 2021].

Gill, P 2020 Of intelligence oversight and the challenge of surveillance corporatism. *Intelligence and National Security*, 35(7): 970–989. DOI: https://doi.org/10.1080/02684527.2020.1783875.

Global Alliance for Reporting Progress on Peaceful, Just and Inclusive Societies 2019 *Enabling the Implementation of the 2030 Agenda through SDG-16+: Anchoring Peace, Justice and Inclusion*. New York: United Nations. Available at: https://www.sdg16hub.org [Last accessed 15 February 2021].

Global Alliance for Reporting Progress on Peaceful, Just and Inclusive Societies 2020 *Who We Are?* Available at: https://www.un-globalalliance.org/about [Last accessed 15 February 2021].

Goodhand, J and **Sedra, M** 2010 Who owns the peace? Aid, reconstruction and peacebuilding in Afghanistan. *Disasters*, 34: 78–102.

Gordon, E 2014 Security sector reform, statebuilding and local ownership: Securing the state or its people? *Journal of Intervention and Statebuilding*, 8(2–3): 126–148.

Grabek, J and **Engwicht, N** 2019 *Enhancing EU Resource Governance Interventions: A Call for Prioritising Human Security*. Johannesburg: South African Institute of International Affairs.

Graff, C 2020 Don't leave fragile states behind in the fight against coronavirus: Fragile states are poorly equipped to deal with an outbreak, posing a significant risk in the global response to COVID-19. *United States Institute of Peace*, 31 March. Available at: https://www.usip.org/pub lications/2020/03/dont-leave-fragile-states-behind-fight-against-coronavirus [Last accessed 15 February 2021].

Grant, R W and **Keohane, R O** 2005 Accountability and abuses of power in world politics. *American Political Science Review*, 99(1): 29–43.

Guerber, T 2018 SSR, prevention and sustaining peace. *DCAF Blog*, 26 June. Available at: https: //www.dcaf.ch/ssr-prevention-and-sustaining-peace [Last accessed 15 February 2021].

Guo, F 2017 The spirit and characteristic of the general provisions of civil law. *Law and Economics*, 3: 5–16.

Hannah, G, O'Brien, K A, and **Rathmell, A** 2005 *Intelligence and Security Legislation for Security Sector Reform*. Technical Report, June. London: RAND Europe.

Hansen, A S 2008 Local ownership in peace operations. In: Timothy, D (ed.) *Local Ownership and Security Sector Reform*. Zürich: Lit Verlag. pp. 39–58.

Harborne, B, Dorotinsky, W, and **Bisca, P M** 2017 Securing development: Public finance and the security sector. Washington, DC: World Bank. Available at: https://openknowledge.world bank.org/handle/10986/25138 [Last accessed 15 February 2021].

Hassan, A M 2020 The impact of corruption on the human security of societies in transition (Iraq case study since 2003). *Review of Economics and Political Science*, ISSN: 2631-3561.

Hänggi, H 2003 making sense of security sector governance. In: Hänggi, H and Winkler, T (eds.) *Challenges of Security Sector Governance*. Geneva: DCAF. pp. 3–23.

Hänggi, H 2009 Security sector reform. In: Chetail, V (ed.) *Post-Conflict Peacebuilding: A Lexicon*. Oxford, UK: Oxford University Press. pp. 337–349.

Heisler, M, Mishori, R, and **Haar, R** 2020 Protests against police violence met by more police violence: A dangerous paradox. *JAMA Network*, 11 June. Available at: https://jamanetwork.com /channels/health-forum/fullarticle/2767270 [Last accessed 12 September 2020].

Hendrickson, D and **Karkoszka, A** 2002 The challenges of security sector reform. *SIPRI Yearbook*. pp. 175–202.

Hill, P S, Mansoor, G F, and **Claudio, F** 2010 Conflict in least-developed countries: Challenging the millennium development goals. *Bulletin of the World Health Organization,* 88(8): 562. DOI: https://doi.org/10.2471/blt.09.071365.

Hope, K R Sr. 2020a Civilian oversight for democratic policing and its challenges: Overcoming obstacles for improved police accountability, *Journal of Applied Security Research.* Published online on 10 July. DOI: https://doi.org/10.1080/19361610.2020.1777807.

Hope, K R Sr. 2020b Peace, justice and inclusive institutions: Overcoming challenges to the implementation of Sustainable Development Goal 16. *Global Change, Peace & Security,* 32(1): 57–77.

Hryniewicz, D 2011 Civilian oversight as a public good: democratic policing, civilian oversight, and the social, *Contemporary Justice Review,* 14(1): 77–83.

Hylton, K N 2019 When should we prefer tort law to environmental regulation? *Washburn Law Journal,* 41: 515–534.

Institute for Economics & Peace (IEP) 2020 *Global Peace Index 2020: Measuring Peace in a Complex World.* Sydney, June. Available at: http://visionofhumanity.org/reports [Last accessed 15 February 2021].

Inter-American Institute of Human Rights 2020 What is human security? Available at: https://www.iidh.ed.cr/multic/default_12.aspx?contenidoid=ea75e2b1-9265-4296-9d8c-3391de83fb42&Portal=IIDHSeguridadEN [Last accessed 15 February 2021].

International Institute for Sustainable Development (IISD) 2016 *Implementing the 2030 Agenda and Its SDGs: Where to Start?* 4 February. Available at: http://sdg.iisd.org/commentary/policy-briefs/implementing-the-2030-agenda-and-its-sdgs-where-to-start/ [Last accessed 15 February 2021].

Jacobs, J 2015 International development patterns, strategies, theories & explanations. *Geography of International Affairs.* Available at: https://www.e-education.psu.edu/geog128/node/719 [Last accessed 15 February 2021].

Justaert, A 2012 The implementation of the EU security sector reform policies in the Democratic Republic of Congo? *European Security,* 21(2): 219–235.

Kanie, N and **Biermann, F** 2017 *Governing Through Goals: Sustainable Development Goals as Governance Innovation.* Cambridge: MIT Press.

Khasanova, L 2020 International relations in the post-COVID-19 era: Cooperation vs. protectionism. *Atlas Institute for International Affairs,* 8 April. Available at: https://www.internationalaffairshouse.org/cooperation-vs-protectionism-in-post-covid-19/ [Last accessed 15 February 2021].

Knudsen, T B and **Laustsen, C B** 2006 *Kosovo Between War and Peace: Nationalism, Peacebuilding and International Trusteeship.* New York: Routledge.

Krause, K and **Jütersonke, O** 2005 Peace, security and development in post-conflict environments. *Security Dialogue,* 36(4): 447–462.

Kunz, R and **Valasek, K** 2012 Learning from others' mistakes: Towards participatory, gender-sensitive SSR. In: Schnabel, A and Farr, V (eds.) *Back to the Roots: Security Sector Reform and Development.* Münster: LIT Verlag. pp. 115–143.

Larivé, Maxime H A 2012. From speeches to actions: EU involvement in the war in Afghanistan through the EUPOL Afghanistan Mission. *European Security,* 21(2): 185–201.

Law, D 2006 Conclusion: Security sector (re)construction in post-conflict settings. *International Peacekeeping,* 13(1): 111–123.

Law, D and **Myshlovska, O** 2008 The evolution of the concepts of security sector reform and security sector governance: The EU perspective.' In: Spence, D and Fluri, P (eds.) *The European Union and Security Sector Reform.* London: John Harper Publishing.

Lazarus, L 2020 Securitizing sustainable development? The coercive sting in SDG16. In: Kaltenborn, M, Krajewski, M, and Kuhn, H (eds.) *Sustainable Development Goals and Human Rights.* Springer Open. pp. 155–170.

Leal Filho, W, Brandli, L L, Lange Salvia, A, Rayman-Bacchus, L and **Platje, J** 2020 COVID-19 and the UN sustainable development goals: Threat to solidarity or an opportunity? *Sustainability*, 12(13): 5343.

Luckham, R 2003 Democratic strategies for security in transition and conflict. In: Cawthra, G and Luckham, R (eds.) *Governing Insecurity*. London and New York: Zed Books. pp. 3–28.

Mac Ginty, R 2008 Indigenous peace-making versus the liberal peace. *Cooperation and Conflict*, 43(2): 139–163.

Mac Ginty, R 2015 Where is the local? Critical localism and peacebuilding. *Third World Quarterly*, 36(5): 840–856.

Maresko, D 2004 Development, relief aid, and creating peace: Humanitarian aid in Liberia's war. *OJPCR: The Online Journal of Peace and Conflict Resolution*, 6(1): 94–120.

Martin, M 2012 Kosovo case study. In: Martin, M and Moser, S (eds.) *Exiting Conflict, Owning the Peace: Local Ownership and Peacebuilding Relationships in the Cases of Bosnia and Kosovo.* London: Friedrich Ebert Stiftung and LSE. pp. 15–22.

Martin, M, Bojicic-Dzelilovic, V, Kostovicova, D, Wittman, A, and **Moser, S** 2012 Local ownership in international peace operations: Conclusions and policy recommendations. In: Martin, M and Moser, S (eds.) *Exiting Conflict, Owning the Peace: Local Ownership and Peacebuilding Relationships in the Cases of Bosnia and Kosovo.* London: Friedrich Ebert Stiftung and LSE. pp. 3–7.

Martin, M and **Owen, T** 2010 The second generation of human security: Lessons from the UN and EU experience. *International Affairs*, 86(1): 211–224.

McCandless, E 2020 Resilient social contracts and peace: Towards a needed reconceptualization, *Journal of Intervention and Statebuilding*, 14(1): 1–21.

Meharg, S, Arnusch, A and **Cook Merrill, S** 2010 *Security Sector Reform: A Case Study Approach to Transition and Capacity Building.* Carlisle, PA: Strategic Studies Institute.

Mensah, J and **Casadevall, S R** 2019 Sustainable development: Meaning, history, principles, pillars, and implications for human action: Literature review. *Cogent Social Sciences*, 5(1): 1–21.

Milante, G, Jang, S, Park, H, and **Ryu, K** 2015 *Goal 16 – The Indicators We Want: Virtual Network Sourcebook on Measuring Peace, Justice and Effective Institutions*, United Nations Development Programme. New York: UNDP.

Moore, A 2014 CSDP police missions: Comparing bottom-up and top-down approaches. *European Foreign Affairs Review*, 19(2): 283–305.

Möller-Loswick, A 2017 Goal 16 is about peace, not hard security. *Saferworld.org.uk*, 12 October. Available at: https://www.saferworld.org.uk/resources/news-and-analysis/post/740-goal-16-is-about-peaceful-change-not-hard-security [Last accessed 15 February 2021].

Myrttinen, H 2019 Security sector governance, security sector reform and gender. *Gender and Security Toolkit #1*. Geneva: DCAF, OSCE/ODIHR, UN Women. Available at: https://www.dcaf.ch/sites/default/files/publications/documents/GSToolkit_Tool-1%20EN%20FINAL_2.pdf [Last accessed 15 February 2021].

Narten, J 2008 Dilemmas of promoting local ownership: The case of postwar Kosovo. In: Paris, R and Sisk, T (eds.) *The Dilemmas of Statebuilding: Confronting the Contradictions of Postwar Peace Operations.* New York: Routledge. pp. 252–284.

Nathan, L 2007 *No Ownership, No Commitment: A Guide to Local Ownership of Security Sector Reform.* Birmingham: University of Birmingham. Available at: http://epapers.bham.ac.uk/1530/1/Nathan_%2D2007%2D_No_Ownership.pdf [Last accessed 15 February 2021].

Newman, E 2016 Human security: Reconciling critical aspirations with political 'realities.' *The British Journal of Criminology*, 56(6): 1165–1183.

Newman, E, Paris, R, and **Richmond, O** (eds) 2009 *New Perspectives on Liberal Peacebuilding.* Tokyo and New York: United Nations University Press.

North, D, Wallis, J and **Weingast, B** 2009 *Violence and Social Orders: A Conceptual Framework for Interpreting Recorded Human History.* New York: Cambridge University Press.

Oberleitner, G 2005 Human security: A challenge to international law? *Global Governance,* 11(2): 185–203.

Organisation for Economic Co-operation and Development (OECD) 2005 *Security System Reform and Governance: A DAC Reference Document.* Paris: OECD Publications. Available at: http://www.oecd.org/dataoecd/8/39/31785288.pdf [Last accessed 15 February 2021].

OECD 2008 *Handbook on Security System Reform: Supporting Security and Justice.* Paris: OECD Publishing.

OECD 2010 *Do No Harm: International Support for Statebuilding.* Conflict and Fragility Series. Paris: OECD Publications. Available at: https://www.oecd.org/dac/conflict-fragility-resilience/docs/do%20no%20harm.pdf [Last accessed 15 February 2021].

OECD 2020a *The DAC Mandate.* Available at: http://www.oecd.org/dac/development-assistance-committee/ [Last accessed 15 February 2021].

OECD 2020b *Official Development Assistance*, April. Available at: http://www.oecd.org/dac/financing-sustainable-development/development-finance-standards/What-is-ODA.pdf [Last accessed 15 February 2021].

Organisation for Economic Co-operation and Development-Development Assistance Committee (OECD-DAC) 2007 *OECD DAC Handbook on Security System Reform (SSR): Supporting Security and Justice.* Paris: OECD.

OECD-DAC 2010 *The State's Legitimacy in Fragile Situations: Unpacking Complexity.* Paris: OECD.

Nilsson, M, Griggs D, and **Visbeck M** 2016 *Policy: Map the interactions between Sustainable Development Goals, Nature*, 15 June. Available at: https://www.nature.com/news/policy-map-the-interactions-between-sustainable-development-goals-1.20075 [Last accessed 15 February 2021].

Paffenholz, T 2014 *Broadening Participation in Peace Processes: Dilemmas and Options for Mediators*, June. Bradford: The Centre for Humanitarian Dialogue.

Papagianni, K 2009 Transitional politics in post-conflict countries: The importance of consultative and inclusive political processes. *Journal of Intervention and Statebuilding*, 3(1): 47–63.

Paris, R 2001 Human security: Paradigm shift or hot air? *International Security*, 26(2): 87–102.

Pathfinders 2020 Act now for SDG16Plus: Peace, justice, inclusion and strong institutions in a pandemic, July. Available at: https://530cfd94-d934-468b-a1c7-c67a84734064.filesusr.com/ugd/6c192f_f93d75d7d34643d1a1528cae6ca88778.pdf [Last accessed 15 February 2021].

Paul B D 2008 A history of the concept of sustainable development: Literature review. *The Annals of the University of Oradea, Economic Sciences Series*, 17(2): 576–580.

Peake, G, Scheye, E and **Hills, A** 2006 Conclusion. *Civil Wars*, 8(2): 251–252.

Peter, M 2013 Whither sovereignty? The limits of building states through international administrations. In: Rudolph, J R Jr. and Lahneman, W J (eds.) *From Mediation to Nation-Building: Third Parties and the Management of Communal Conflict.* Lanham, MD: Rowman and Littlefield. pp. 419–438.

Poast, P 2020 COVID 2025: Changing the rules of international relations. UChicago News Interview, 27 April. Available at: https://news.uchicago.edu/videos/covid-2025-changing-rules-international-relations-paul-poast [Last accessed 15 February 2021].

Portada, R A, Riley, J H, and **Gambone, M D** 2014 Security sector reform in South Sudan: Identifying roles for private military and security companies. *Journal of Third World Studies*, 31(2): 151–178.

PreventionWeb 2020 The human security network. Available at: https://www.preventionweb.net/organizations/17066/view [Last accessed 15 February 2021].

Pugh, M, Cooper, N, and **Turner, M** (eds.) 2008 *Whose Peace? Critical Perspectives on the Political Economy of Peacebuilding.* Basingstoke: Palgrave MacMillan.

Pupavac, V 2010 The consumerism-development-security nexus. *Security Dialogue,* 41(6): 691–713.

Quirk, P 2020 The global fragility strategy: Posturing the United States for a reshaping world order. *Brookings,* 15 May. Available at: https://www.brookings.edu/blog/order-from-chaos /2020/05/15/the-global-fragility-strategy-posturing-the-united-states-for-a-reshaping-world -order/ [Last accessed 15 February 2021].

Radović, V 2019 *SDG-16: Peace and Justice: Challenges, Actions and the Way Forward.* Bingley, UK: Emerald Publishing Limited.

Rice S E 2003 The new National Security Strategy: Focus on failed states. *The Brookings Institution Policy Brief* #116, February. Available at: https://www.brookings.edu/wp-content /uploads/2016/06/pb116.pdf [Last accessed 15 February 2021].

Richards, A and **Smith, H** 2007 Addressing the role of private security companies within security sector reform programmes. *Journal of Security Sector Management,* 5(1): 1–14.

Richmond, O P 2006 The problem of peace: Understanding the 'liberal peace'. *Conflict, Security & Development,* 6(3): 291–314.

Rocha Menocal, A 2015 *Inclusive Political Settlements: Evidence, Gaps, and Challenges of Institutional Transformation.* Birmingham, UK: International Development Department, University of Birmingham.

Rostow, W W 1971 *The Stages of Economic Growth: A Non-Communist Manifesto.* Cambridge: Cambridge University Press.

Rüland, J, Manea, M G, Born, H (eds.) 2012 *The Politics of Military Reform: Experiences from Indonesia and Nigeria.* Heidelberg: Springer Science & Business Media.

Sachs, J, Schmidt-Traub, G, Kroll, C, Lafortune, G, Fuller, G 2019 *Sustainable Development Report 2019.* New York: Bertelsmann Stiftung and Sustainable Development Solutions Network (SDSN).

Scheye, E 2008a UNMIK and the significance of effective programme management: The case of Kosovo. In: Hänggi, H and Scherrer, V (eds.) *Security Sector Reform and UN Integrated Missions* Geneva: DCAF. pp. 169–219.

Scheye, E 2008b Unknotting local ownership redux: Bringing non-state/local justice networks back. In: Donais, T (ed.) *Local Ownership and Security Sector Reform.* DCAF Yearbook. Münster: LIT Verlag. pp. 59–81.

Schnabel, A 2012 The security-development discourse and the role of SSR as a development instrument. In: Schnabel, A and Farr, V (eds.) *Back to the Roots: Security Sector Reform and Development.* Münster: LIT Verlag. pp. 29–76.

Schnabel, A and **Farr, V** (eds.) 2012 *Back to the Roots: Security Sector Reform and Development.* Münster: LIT Verlag.

Schulz, S and **Yeung, C** 2008 *Private Military and Security Companies and Gender.* Geneva: DCAF.

Schwarz, R 2005 Post-conflict peacebuilding: The challenges of security, welfare, and representation. *Security Dialogue,* 36(4): 429–446.

SDG-16 Conference 2019 Outcome: Key messages and recommendations. Conference in preparation for HLPF 2019, organized by the UN Department of Economic and Social Affairs (DESA) and the International Development Law Organization (IDLO) with the Government of Italy, 27–29 May. Available at: https://sustainabledevelopment.un.org/content /documents/23814SDG_16_MAIN_SUMMARY_SDG_Conference_Rome_May2019.pdf [Last accessed 15 February 2021].

Sedra, M 2006a European approaches to security sector reform: Examining trends through the lens of Afghanistan. *European Security,* 15(3): 323–338.

Sedra, M 2006b Security sector reform in Afghanistan: The slide towards expediency. *International Peacekeeping*, 13(1): 94–110.

Sedra, M 2010 Security sector reform 101: Understanding the concept, charting trends and identifying challenges. Report, *The Center for International Governance Innovation* (CIGI). Available at: https://www.cigionline.org/sites/default/files/ssr_101_final_april_27.pdf [Last accessed 15 February 2021].

Shani, G 2007 'Democratic imperialism,' 'neoliberal globalization' and human in/security in the Global South. In: Shani, G, Sato, M, Pasha, M K (eds.) *Protecting Human Security in a Post 9/11 World*. London: Palgrave Macmillan, London. pp. 17–29.

Short, C 2014 Foreword. In: Dursun-Özkanca, O (ed.) 2014 *The European Union as an Actor in Security Sector Reform: Current Practices and Challenges of Implementation*. New York: Routledge. p. ix.

Simons, G 2012 Security sector reform and Georgia: The European Union's challenge in the Southern Caucasus. *European Security*, 21(2): 272–293.

Solar, C 2019 Civil-military relations and human security in a post-dictatorship. *Journal of Strategic Studies*, 42(3–4): 507–531.

Spence, D and **Fluri, P** (eds.) 2008 *The European Union and Security Sector Reform*. London: John Harper Publishing.

Steiner, A 2019 25th Anniversary of the human security concept. Keynote speech: Reflections on the past 25 years since the Human Development Report of 1994 and discuss the contribution the human security approach has made to the achievement of the SDGs, 28 February. Available at: https://www.undp.org/content/undp/en/home/news-centre/speeches/2019/25th-anniversary-of-the-human-security-concept.html [Last accessed 15 February 2021].

Stern, M and **Öjendal, J** 2010 Mapping the security-development nexus: Conflict, complexity, cacophony, convergence? *Security Dialogue*, 41(1): 5–29.

Stewart, F (ed.) 2008 *Horizontal Inequalities and Conflict: Understanding Group Violence in Multi-ethnic Societies*. London: Palgrave Macmillan.

Sumner, A, Ortiz-Juarez, E and **Hoy, C** 2020 Precarity and the pandemic: COVID-19 and poverty incidence, intensity, and severity in developing countries. *WIDER Working Paper* 2020/77. Helsinki: UNU-WIDER.

Tadesse, M 2010 *The African Union and Security Sector Reform: A Review of the Post-Conflict Development and Reconstruction (PCRD) Policy*. Addis Ababa: Friedrich Ebert Stiftung.

Tadjbakhsh, S 2013 In defense of the broad view of human security. In: Martin, M and Owen, T (eds.) *Routledge Handbook of Human Security*. New York: Routledge. pp. 43–57.

Tavanti, M and **Stachowicz-Stanusch, A** 2013 Sustainable solutions for human security and anti-corruption: Integrating theories and practices. *International Journal of Sustainable Human Security*, 1(1): 1–21.

Temple-Raston, D 2020 Watchdog to review nonlethal tactics against protesters, including 'heat ray' request. *National Public Radio*, 18 September. Available at: https://www.npr.org/2020/09/18/914409368/watchdog-to-review-non-lethal-tactics-against-protesters-including-heat-ray-requ [Last accessed 15 February 2021].

Thede, N 2013 Policy coherence for development and securitisation: Competing paradigms or stabilising North–South hierarchies? *Third World Quarterly*, 34(5): 784–799.

Tougas, M L 2009 Some comments and observations on the Montreux Document. *Yearbook of International Humanitarian Law* 12: 321–345.

Transparency, Accountability and Participation Network 2016 Goal 16 advocacy toolkit: A practical guide for stakeholders for national-level advocacy around peaceful, just and inclusive societies. Available at: https://sustainabledevelopment.un.org/content/documents/9935TAP%20Network%20Goal%2016%20Advocacy%20Toolkit.pdf [Last accessed 15 February 2021].

Tricot O'Farrell, K 2016 EU foreign policy risks fuelling displacement and terror. *Saferworld*, 22 August. Available at: https://www.saferworld.org.uk/resources/news-and-analysis/post/203 -eu-foreign-policy-will-fuel-displacement-and-terror-unless-it-focuses-on-what-is-driving -them [Last accessed 15 February 2021].

Tschirgi, N 2005 Security and development policies: Untangling the relationship. Paper prepared for the European Association of Development Research and Training Institutes (EADI) Conference, Bonn, September. Available at: http://gsdrc.org/docs/open/cc108.pdf [Last accessed 15 February 2021].

Tholens, S 2012 Which and whose authority? EU support to security governance in Aceh. *European Security*, 21(2): 294–309.

Tosun, J and **Leininger, J** 2017 Governing the interlinkages between the sustainable development goals: Approaches to attain policy integration. *Global Challenges*, 1(9):1–12.

United Kingdom Department for International Development (DFID) 2002 *Understanding and Supporting Security Sector Reform*. London. Available at: https://www.securitycouncilreport .org/atf/cf/%7B65BFCF9B-6D27-4E9C-8CD3-CF6E4FF96FF9%7D/supportingsecurity[1] .pdf [Last accessed 15 February 2021].

United Kingdom Department for International Development (DFID) 2009 *Eliminating World Poverty: Building Our Common Future*. CM7656, London, July. Available at: https://assets .publishing.service.gov.uk/government/uploads/system/uploads/attachment_data/file /229029/7656.pdf [Last accessed 15 February 2021].

United Nations 2015 *Millennium Development Goals Report*. New York: United Nations. Available at: https://www.un.org/millenniumgoals/2015_MDG_Report/pdf/MDG%202015%20rev %20(July%201).pdf [Last accessed on 15 February 2021].

United Nations 2018 Deputy-Secretary General Report. Security sector reform 'a core element' of prevention, sustaining peace agendas, says Deputy Secretary-General at High-Level round table. DSG/SM/1168, 23 April. Available at: https://www.un.org/press/en/2018/dsgsm1168 .doc.htm [Last accessed 15 February 2021].

United Nations 2020a *Goal 16: Promote Just, Peaceful and Inclusive Societies*. Available at: https: //www.un.org/sustainabledevelopment/peace-justice/ [Last accessed 15 February 2021].

United Nations 2020b *Covid-19 Response: Financing for Development in the Era of COVID-19 and Beyond*. Available at: https://www.un.org/en/coronavirus/financing-development [Last accessed 15 February 2021].

United Nations 2020c *Shared Responsibility, Global Solidarity: Responding to the Socio-Economic Impacts of COVID-19*. March. New York: United Nations. Available at: https://unsdg.un.org /sites/default/files/2020-03/SG-Report-Socio-Economic-Impact-of-Covid19.pdf [Last accessed 15 February 2021].

United Nations and **World Bank** 2018 *Pathways for Peace: Inclusive Approaches to Preventing Violent Conflict*. Washington DC: World Bank.

United Nations Department of Peacekeeping Operations 2012 *The United Nations SSR Perspective*. Office of Rule of Law and Security Institutions, Security Sector Reform Unit. New York: United Nations. Available at: https://peacekeeping.un.org/sites/default/files/ssr_perspective _2012.pdf [Last accessed 15 February 2021].

United Nations Development Programme 1994 New dimensions of human security. *Human Development Report 1994*. New York: Oxford University Press. Available at: http://hdr.undp .org/sites/default/files/reports/255/hdr_1994_en_complete_nostats.pdf [Last accessed 15 February 2021].

United Nations Development Programme 2016 UNDP support to the implementation of the 2030 Agenda for Sustainable Development. *UNDP Policy and Programme Brief*, January. Available at: https://www.undp.org/content/undp/en/home/librarypage/sustainable-development

-goals/strategy-undp-support-to-the-implementation-of-the-2030-agenda/ [Last accessed 15 February 2021].

United Nations Development Programme 2017 Monitoring to implement peaceful, just and inclusive societies: Pilot initiative on national-level monitoring of SDG16. Oslo, Norway: UNDP.

United Nations Development Programme Brussels 2017 Goal 16: Peace, justice and strong institutions. Available at: https://www.undp.org/content/brussels/en/home/sustainable-development-goals/goal-16-peace-justice-and-strong-institutions.html [Last accessed 15 February 2021].

United Nations Development Programme and Oxford Policy Management 2019 *Do Fragile and Conflict-Affected Countries Prioritise Core Government Functions?* New York, NY: UNDP. Available at: file:///Users/dursuno/Downloads/CGFs%2520in%2520FCAS%2520Combined%2520Report_v1.1-web.pdf [Last accessed 15 February 2021].

United Nations General Assembly 2004 Note by the Secretary-General. 2 December. A/59/565.

United Nations General Assembly 2012 Resolution 66/290. Follow-up to paragraph 143 on human security of the 2005 World Summit Outcome, 25 October. A/Res/66/290.

United Nations General Assembly 2013 Resolution 68/685. Follow-up to General Assembly resolution 66/290 on human security, 23 December. A/Res/68/685.

United Nations General Assembly 2015 Resolution 70/1. Transforming our world: The 2030 agenda for sustainable development, 21 October. A/Res/70/1.

United Nations General Assembly 2016 Resolution 70/299. Follow-up and review of the 2030 Agenda for Sustainable Development at the global level, 18 August. A/Res/70/299.

United Nations High Commissioner on Refugees 2020 Global trends: Forced displacement in 2019. Available at: https://www.unhcr.org/globaltrends2019/ [Last accessed 15 February 2021].

United Nations Millennium Declaration 2000 Millennium summit of the United Nations, 6–8 September. Available at: https://www.un.org/en/development/devagenda/millennium.shtml [Last accessed 15 February 2021].

United Nations Millennium Project 2005 Investing in development: A practical plan to achieve the Millennium Development Goals. Overview. Communications Development Inc: New York.

United Nations Office on Drugs and Crime (UNODC) 2012 Member States express strong support for 'One-UN' approach of UNODC and other partners to transnational organized crime and drug trafficking. February. Available at: https://www.unodc.org/unodc/en/frontpage/2012/February/member-states-express-strong-support-forone-un-approach-by-unodc-and-other-partners-on-transnational-organized-crime-and-drug-trafficking.html [Last accessed 15 February 2021].

United Nations Peacekeeping 2020 Security sector reform. Available at: https://peacekeeping.un.org/en/security-sector-reform [Last accessed 15 February 2021].

United Nations Secretary-General 1992 Report of the Secretary-General. *An Agenda for Peace: Preventive Diplomacy, Peacemaking and Peace-keeping*, 31 January. A/47/277–S/24111.

United Nations Secretary-General 1994 Report of the Secretary-General. *An Agenda for Development*, 6 May. A/48/935.

United Nations Secretary-General 2001 Report of the Secretary-General. *No exit without strategy: Security Council decision-making and the closure or transition of United Nations peacekeeping operations*, 20 April. S/2001/394.

United Nations Secretary-General 2005 Report of the Secretary-General. *In Larger Freedom: Towards Development, Security and Human Rights for All*, 21 March. A/59/2005.

United Nations Secretary-General 2008 Report of the Secretary-General. *Securing Peace and Development: The Role of the United Nations in Supporting Security Sector Reform*, 23 January. A/62/659 S/2008/39.

United Nations Secretary-General 2013 Report of the Secretary-General. *Securing States and Societies: Strengthening the United Nations Comprehensive Support to Security Sector Reform,* 13 August. A/67/970 S/2013/480.

United Nations Secretary-General 2019 Report of the Secretary-General on the work of the organization. New York: United Nations. A/74/1.

United Nations Security Council 2020a Letter from the Permanent Representative of South Africa to the United Nations addressed to the Secretary-General. 25 November. New York: United Nations. S/2020/1145.

United Nations Security Council 2020b Resolution 2553. 3 December. New York: United Nations. S/Res/2553.

United Nations Statistics Division 2016 Goal 16 Promote peaceful and inclusive societies for sustainable development, provide access to justice for all and build effective, accountable and inclusive institutions at all levels, 3 March. Available at: https://unstats.un.org/sdgs/files /metadata-compilation/Metadata-Goal-16.pdf [Last accessed 15 February 2021].

United Nations Trust Fund for Human Security (UNTFHS) 2016 *Human Security Handbook.* Human Security Unit, January. Available at: https://www.un.org/humansecurity/wp-content /uploads/2017/10/h2.pdf [Last accessed 15 February 2021].

United Nations Trust Fund for Human Security (UNTFHS) 2020 What's new: 19 June 2020 – Virtual panel on 'Human security: A unifying framework to address 21st century challenges.' Available at: https://www.un.org/humansecurity/whats-new/ [Last accessed 15 February 2021].

United Nations Women 2020 COVID-19: Gendered impacts of the pandemic in Palestine and implications for policy and programming, April. Available at: https://www2.unwomen.org/- /media/field%20office%20palestine/attachments/publications/2020/4/covid%2019%20-%20un %20women%20rapid%20gender%20analysis.pdf?la=en&vs=4626 [Last accessed 15 February 2021].

United States Agency for International Development (USAID) 2020 *The Effectiveness of Police Accountability Mechanisms and Programs: What Works and The Way Ahead.* August. Available at: https://www.usaid.gov/sites/default/files/documents/Police_Accountability_Mechanisms _8.5.2020.pdf [Last accessed 15 February 2021].

United States Department of State Bulletin 1944 The International Bank for Reconstruction and Development. Volume 11(2), July. p. 2.

Uvin, P 1998 *Aiding Violence: The Development Enterprise in Rwanda.* West Hartford, CT: Kumarian.

Vandemoortele, A 2012 Adaptation, resistance and a (re)turn to functionalism: The case of the Bosnian police restructuring process (2003–2008). *European Security,* 21(2): 202–218.

Vetschra, H and **Damian, M** 2006 Security sector reform in Bosnia and Herzegovina: The role of the international community. *International Peacekeeping,* 13(1): 28–42.

Vos, R, Martin, W and **Laborde, D** 2020 How much will global poverty increase because of COVID-19? International Food Policy Research Institute Blog, 20 March. Available at: https://www.ifpri.org/blog/how-much-will-global-poverty-increase-because-covid-19 [Last accessed 15 February 2021].

Waage, J, Banerji, R, Campbell, O, Chirwa, E, Collender, G, Dieltiens, V, and **Unterhalter, E** 2010 The millennium development goals: A cross-sectoral analysis and principles for goal setting after 2015. *Lancet,* 376(9745): 991–1023.

Walter, B F 2014 Why bad governance leads to repeat civil war. *Journal of Conflict Resolution,* 59(7): 1242–1272.

Weitz, N, Carlsen, H, Nilsson, M, and **Skånberg, K** 2017 Towards systemic and contextual priority setting for implementing the 2030 Agenda. *Sustainability Science,* 13(2): 531–548. DOI: https://doi.org/10.1007/s11625-017-0470-0.

Werthes, S, Heaven, C, and **Vollnhals, S** 2011 Assessing human insecurity worldwide: The way to a human (in)security index. *Institute for Development and Peace*, INEF Report, 102. Available at: http://edoc.vifapol.de/opus/volltexte/2013/4867/pdf/report102.pdf [Last accessed 15 February 2021].

Winkler, T 2012 Preface. In: Schnabel, A and Farr, V (eds.), *Back to the Roots: Security Sector Reform and Development*. Münster: LIT Verlag.

Wolff, S and **Dursun-Özkanca, O** 2012 Regional and international conflict regulation: Diplomatic, economic and military interventions. *Civil Wars*, 14(3): 297–323, DOI: https://doi.org/10.1080/13698249.2012.706948

World Bank 2003 *Breaking the Conflict Trap: Civil War and Development Policy*. World Bank Policy Research Report. Washington DC: World Bank.

World Bank 2011 *World Development Report 2011: Conflict, Security, and Development*. Washington DC: World Bank.

World Commission on Environment and Development (WCED) 1987 *Our Common Future*. Available at: https://sustainabledevelopment.un.org/content/documents/5987our-common-future.pdf [Last accessed 15 February 2021].

Wulf, H 2004 *Security Sector Reform in Developing and Transitional Countries*. Berlin: Berghof Research Center for Constructive Conflict Management, July. Available at: http://www.berghof-handbook.net/documents/publications/dialogue2_wulf.pdf [Last accessed 15 February 2021].

Wulf, H 2011 Security sector reform in developing and transitional countries. In: Austin, B, Fischer, M, Giessmann, H J (eds.) 2011 *Advancing Conflict Transformation*. The Berghof Handbook II. Opladen/Framington Hills: Barbara Budrich Publishers. pp. 337–357.

Wunsch, N 2020 How Covid-19 is deepening democratic backsliding and geopolitical competition in the Western Balkans. LSE European Politics and Policy (EUROPP) Blog, 20 May. Available at: http://eprints.lse.ac.uk/104829/ [Last accessed 15 February 2021].

Zeigermann, U 2020 Policy coherence for sustainable development: A promising approach for human security in fragile states. *Journal of Peacebuilding & Development*, 1542316620909077.

Zhai, T T and **Chang, Y C** 2019 Standing of environmental public-interest litigants in China: Evolution, obstacles and solutions. *Journal of Environmental Law*, 30, 369–397. DOI: https://doi.org/10.1093/jel/eqy011.

Ziai, A 2011 The millennium development goals: Back to the future? *Third World Quarterly*, 3(1): 27–43. DOI: https://doi.org/10.1080/01436597.2011.543811.

Zoellick, R 2008 Fragile states: Securing development. Speech prepared for delivery at The International Institute for Strategic Studies, Geneva, 12 September. Available at: http://documents.worldbank.org/curated/en/573741523266673715/pdf/Fragile-states-securing-development-by-Robert-B-Zoellick-President-The-World-Bank-Group.pdf [Last accessed 15 February 2021].

www.ingramcontent.com/pod-product-compliance
Lightning Source LLC
Chambersburg PA
CBHW041425270326
41931CB00022B/3490